CLOUD SECURITY & FORENSICS HANDBOOK

DIVE DEEP INTO AZURE, AWS, AND GCP

4 BOOKS IN 1

BOOK 1
CLOUD SECURITY ESSENTIALS: A BEGINNER'S GUIDE TO AZURE, AWS, AND GCP

BOOK 2
MASTERING CLOUD SECURITY: ADVANCED STRATEGIES FOR AZURE, AWS, AND GCP

BOOK 3
CLOUD SECURITY AND FORENSICS: INVESTIGATING INCIDENTS IN AZURE, AWS, AND GCP

BOOK 4
EXPERT CLOUD SECURITY AND COMPLIANCE AUTOMATION: AZURE, AWS, AND GCP BEST PRACTICES

ROB BOTWRIGHT

Published by Rob Botwright
Library of Congress Cataloging-in-Publication Data
ISBN 978-1-83938-564-3
Cover design by Rizzo

Disclaimer

The contents of this book are based on extensive research and the best available historical sources. However, the author and publisher make no claims, promises, or guarantees about the accuracy, completeness, or adequacy of the information contained herein. The information in this book is provided on an "as is" basis, and the author and publisher disclaim any and all liability for any errors, omissions, or inaccuracies in the information or for any actions taken in reliance on such information.

The opinions and views expressed in this book are those of the author and do not necessarily reflect the official policy or position of any organization or individual mentioned in this book. Any reference to specific people, places, or events is intended only to provide historical context and is not intended to defame or malign any group, individual, or entity. The information in this book is intended for educational and entertainment purposes only. It is not intended to be a substitute for professional advice or judgment. Readers are encouraged to conduct their own research and to seek professional advice where appropriate.

Every effort has been made to obtain necessary permissions and acknowledgments for all images and other copyrighted material used in this book. Any errors or omissions in this regard are unintentional, and the author and publisher will correct them in future editions.

TABLE OF CONTENTS – BOOK 1 - CLOUD SECURITY ESSENTIALS: A BEGINNER'S GUIDE TO AZURE, AWS, AND GCP

TABLE OF CONTENTS – BOOK 2 - MASTERING CLOUD SECURITY: ADVANCED STRATEGIES FOR AZURE, AWS, AND GCP

TABLE OF CONTENTS – BOOK 3 - CLOUD SECURITY AND FORENSICS: INVESTIGATING INCIDENTS IN AZURE, AWS, AND GCP

TABLE OF CONTENTS – BOOK 4 - EXPERT CLOUD SECURITY AND COMPLIANCE AUTOMATION: AZURE, AWS, AND GCP BEST PRACTICES

Introduction

Welcome to the "Cloud Security & Forensics Handbook: Dive Deep into Azure, AWS, and GCP," a comprehensive guide that takes you on a journey through the intricacies of cloud security and forensics within three of the world's leading cloud platforms: Azure, AWS, and GCP. This book bundle, comprised of four distinct volumes, covers a wide spectrum of topics, from the essentials of cloud security to advanced strategies, incident investigation, and automation best practices.

In today's rapidly evolving digital landscape, cloud computing has revolutionized the way organizations operate. It has ushered in unprecedented scalability, flexibility, and efficiency, enabling businesses to innovate and grow at a remarkable pace. However, this digital transformation has also given rise to new challenges and vulnerabilities, making robust cloud security and effective forensics crucial components of any organization's strategy.

As organizations increasingly migrate their data, applications, and infrastructure to the cloud, there is a growing need for professionals who can navigate this complex ecosystem, ensuring that it remains secure and resilient against emerging threats. This book bundle is designed to empower readers with the knowledge and skills necessary to safeguard their cloud environments effectively.

Book 1: Cloud Security Essentials: A Beginner's Guide to Azure, AWS, and GCP Our journey begins with the foundational principles of cloud security. In this volume, we demystify the cloud landscape for beginners and delve into essential concepts such as the shared responsibility model, identity and access management, encryption, and compliance. Whether you are new to cloud security or seeking to solidify your understanding, this book equips you with the fundamentals needed to build a secure cloud foundation.

Book 2: Mastering Cloud Security: Advanced Strategies for Azure, AWS, and GCP Building on the knowledge gained in the first book, we venture into advanced strategies for securing your cloud resources. From network segmentation to microsegmentation, from security as code to DevSecOps integration, this volume explores cutting-edge approaches that will elevate your cloud security posture. By mastering these advanced techniques, you will be better prepared to defend against sophisticated threats.

Book 3: Cloud Security and Forensics: Investigating Incidents in Azure, AWS, and GCP In the world of cloud computing, incident investigation is a critical skill. Book 3 focuses on digital forensics techniques tailored to cloud environments, guiding you through the process of collecting, analyzing, and preserving digital evidence. Whether you are dealing with data breaches or security incidents, this book equips you with the tools to conduct effective investigations and minimize damage.

Book 4: Expert Cloud Security and Compliance Automation: Azure, AWS, and GCP Best Practices Automation is the future of cloud security and compliance. Book 4 is your guide to implementing automation in your cloud security practices. From security policy as code to compliance scanning and orchestration, you will learn how to streamline and enhance security operations. By automating security and compliance tasks, you can achieve consistency, efficiency, and resilience in your cloud environment.

This book bundle is designed to cater to a wide range of readers, from beginners looking to establish a solid foundation in cloud security to experts seeking to stay ahead of evolving threats and embrace automation. Whether you are a cloud architect, security professional, compliance officer, or digital forensics investigator, the insights and strategies presented in these volumes are invaluable resources in your journey toward securing and investigating the cloud environments of Azure, AWS, and GCP.

So, let us embark on this comprehensive exploration of cloud security and forensics, equipping ourselves to meet the challenges of today's dynamic digital landscape. Whether you are just starting your journey or are a seasoned professional, there is something here for everyone. Together, we will dive deep into the fascinating world of cloud security and forensics, ensuring that the cloud remains a safe and resilient space for innovation and growth.

BOOK 1
CLOUD SECURITY ESSENTIALS
A BEGINNER'S GUIDE TO AZURE, AWS, AND GCP

ROB BOTWRIGHT

Chapter 1: Introduction to Cloud Computing

Cloud computing concepts form the foundation of modern IT infrastructure, enabling organizations to access and utilize resources and services over the internet. In this chapter, we will delve into the fundamental principles and ideas that underpin cloud computing, providing a clear understanding of its significance in today's technology landscape.

At its core, cloud computing is a paradigm that involves the delivery of computing resources, such as servers, storage, databases, networking, software, and more, over the internet. This approach contrasts with traditional on-premises IT infrastructure, where organizations manage and maintain physical servers and hardware within their own data centers.

One of the key advantages of cloud computing is its scalability, allowing businesses to easily scale their resources up or down based on their needs. This elasticity is achieved through virtualization, a technology that creates virtual instances of computing resources from physical hardware.

Cloud computing encompasses various service models, each catering to different needs and levels of management. Infrastructure as a Service (IaaS) provides the fundamental building blocks of computing infrastructure, such as virtual machines, storage, and networking. Platform as a Service (PaaS) offers a higher level of abstraction, enabling developers to build and deploy applications without managing the underlying infrastructure.

Software as a Service (SaaS) delivers fully functional software applications over the internet, eliminating the need for users to install or maintain software on their devices. These service models, collectively known as the cloud service stack, provide a range of options for businesses to choose from based on their requirements.

Another crucial aspect of cloud computing is the deployment model, which defines how and where cloud resources are hosted. Public clouds are operated by cloud service providers and are available to the general public. In contrast, private clouds are dedicated to a single organization and can be hosted on-premises or by a third-party provider. Hybrid clouds combine elements of both public and private clouds, offering greater flexibility and data control.

Cloud computing relies on a shared responsibility model, where the cloud provider is responsible for the security and maintenance of the underlying infrastructure, while customers are responsible for securing their applications and data. This shared responsibility underscores the importance of understanding and implementing robust security practices in the cloud.

Cloud computing's benefits extend beyond scalability and flexibility. It also promotes cost efficiency by eliminating the need for large upfront capital expenditures on hardware and reducing operational costs through automation. Additionally, it enables geographic flexibility, allowing users to access resources from anywhere with an internet connection.

Despite its numerous advantages, cloud computing also presents challenges and considerations. These include data privacy concerns, compliance with regulatory requirements, and potential vendor lock-in. Organizations must carefully assess these factors when adopting cloud services.

As cloud computing continues to evolve, it has given rise to specialized cloud offerings, such as serverless computing and containerization. Serverless computing abstracts server management entirely, enabling developers to focus solely on writing code, while containers package applications and their dependencies into portable, isolated units.

In summary, understanding the fundamental concepts of cloud computing is essential for anyone seeking to leverage its capabilities. Whether you are an IT professional, a business leader, or an aspiring developer, a solid grasp of these concepts will empower you to make informed decisions and harness the full potential of cloud technology.

Cloud computing offers a multitude of benefits that have transformed the way businesses operate in today's digital landscape.

One of the primary advantages of cloud computing is scalability, which enables organizations to easily adjust their computing resources according to their needs.

This flexibility eliminates the need for upfront capital investment in physical hardware and allows businesses to pay for only the resources they use, optimizing cost efficiency.

Furthermore, cloud computing offers the advantage of geographic flexibility, allowing users to access applications and data from virtually anywhere with an internet connection.

This accessibility promotes remote work, collaboration, and business continuity, especially in times when physical office spaces may be inaccessible.

Another significant benefit of the cloud is rapid deployment.

With traditional on-premises infrastructure, acquiring and provisioning hardware and software can be a time-consuming process, often taking weeks or even months.

In contrast, cloud resources can be provisioned within minutes, enabling organizations to respond swiftly to changing market demands.

Cloud providers also manage the underlying infrastructure, including hardware maintenance, software updates, and security patches.

This offloads the burden of infrastructure management from organizations, allowing them to focus on their core business objectives.

Security is a paramount concern for businesses, and cloud providers invest heavily in security measures to protect their infrastructure and customers' data.

They employ advanced security practices, encryption, access controls, and monitoring to ensure data confidentiality and integrity.

This shared responsibility model means that cloud users are responsible for securing their own applications and data within the cloud environment.

Cloud providers offer a range of security tools and services to assist customers in this regard.

The cloud's collaborative nature fosters seamless teamwork and communication.

Employees can access shared documents and applications, collaborate in real-time, and communicate effectively, regardless of their physical location.

Furthermore, the cloud facilitates disaster recovery and business continuity planning.

Data backups, redundancy, and failover mechanisms are built into cloud infrastructures, minimizing the risk of data loss and downtime.

This resilience ensures that businesses can quickly recover from unexpected events, such as hardware failures or natural disasters.

Cloud computing also promotes innovation by providing access to cutting-edge technologies and services.

Developers can leverage cloud resources to experiment, develop, and deploy new applications and services more rapidly.

This agility allows businesses to stay competitive in a fast-paced digital landscape.

In addition to innovation, the cloud enables businesses to access and leverage vast amounts of data.

Data analytics and machine learning services on the cloud provide valuable insights, enabling data-driven decision-making and improving business outcomes.

Moreover, the cloud fosters a green approach to computing.

By consolidating resources and optimizing server utilization, cloud providers can operate more efficiently, reducing the environmental impact of data centers.

Organizations that migrate to the cloud often find that they can reduce their carbon footprint and energy consumption.

However, it's essential to note that while cloud computing offers numerous benefits, it also presents challenges and considerations.

Data privacy and compliance with regulatory requirements are significant concerns for organizations storing sensitive data in the cloud.

Businesses must navigate a complex landscape of data protection laws and regulations to ensure they meet their legal obligations.

Additionally, the cloud introduces the risk of vendor lock-in, where an organization becomes heavily reliant on a specific cloud provider's services and technologies.

To mitigate this risk, businesses can adopt multi-cloud strategies, leveraging multiple cloud providers to maintain flexibility and avoid dependence on a single vendor.

In summary, the benefits of cloud computing are extensive, from scalability and cost efficiency to security and innovation.

It has transformed the way organizations operate, allowing them to adapt to changing market conditions, enhance collaboration, and drive business growth.

While challenges exist, careful planning and adherence to best practices can help organizations maximize the advantages of cloud computing while mitigating potential risks.

By embracing the cloud's capabilities, businesses can position themselves for success in the digital age.

Chapter 2: The Importance of Cloud Security

Security concerns in the cloud are a critical aspect of cloud computing that must be thoroughly understood and addressed.

While cloud computing offers numerous advantages, such as scalability and cost efficiency, it also introduces unique security challenges.

One of the primary concerns is data security, as organizations entrust their sensitive and confidential data to cloud service providers.

This data includes customer information, financial records, intellectual property, and more.

The shared responsibility model in cloud computing means that while cloud providers secure the underlying infrastructure, customers are responsible for protecting their data and applications.

Inadequate access controls and misconfigurations can lead to data breaches, making it essential for organizations to implement robust security measures.

Identity and access management (IAM) play a pivotal role in cloud security.

Managing user identities, enforcing strong authentication, and configuring appropriate access permissions are critical to preventing unauthorized access to cloud resources.

Cloud providers offer IAM tools and services to assist organizations in managing access effectively.

Another significant security concern in the cloud is the risk of unauthorized data exposure.

This can occur through misconfigured storage buckets, publicly accessible APIs, or weak encryption practices.

Organizations must diligently assess their cloud configurations and implement encryption to protect data both at rest and in transit.

Moreover, compliance with industry-specific regulations and data protection laws is a concern for businesses that operate in regulated environments.

Ensuring that cloud operations align with these requirements is vital to avoid legal and financial consequences.

Cloud providers often offer compliance certifications and resources to assist organizations in meeting these obligations.

Cloud security extends beyond data protection to include network security.

Organizations must safeguard their cloud networks from cyber threats, such as distributed denial of service (DDoS) attacks and intrusion attempts.

This requires the implementation of firewalls, intrusion detection and prevention systems (IDPS), and security monitoring.

Vulnerabilities in cloud-based applications and services can be exploited by attackers to gain unauthorized access or execute malicious code.

Regular vulnerability assessments and patch management are crucial to mitigate these risks.

Furthermore, the complexity of cloud environments can pose challenges in terms of visibility and control.

Without adequate monitoring and auditing, security incidents may go unnoticed.

Organizations should implement comprehensive monitoring and logging practices to detect and respond to security events promptly.

Incident response plans are essential for addressing security incidents effectively.

These plans should outline the steps to be taken in the event of a security breach, including containment, investigation, and recovery.

Regular testing of these plans through simulated exercises helps ensure that the organization is prepared to respond to real-world incidents.

In addition to external threats, insider threats must also be considered.

Employees and authorized users with access to cloud resources can inadvertently or intentionally compromise security.

Organizations should implement user behavior analytics and anomaly detection to identify unusual activities that may indicate insider threats.

Security concerns also extend to the management of encryption keys and the protection of cryptographic assets.

Key management practices should be robust to prevent unauthorized access to sensitive information.

The cloud security landscape is continually evolving, with new threats and vulnerabilities emerging regularly.

Staying informed about the latest security trends and best practices is essential for maintaining a secure cloud environment.

Collaboration with cloud providers, security experts, and the broader security community can be valuable in addressing these evolving threats.

In summary, security concerns in the cloud are multifaceted and require a proactive and holistic approach.

Organizations must prioritize security by implementing strong access controls, encryption, monitoring, and incident response plans.

By addressing these concerns effectively, businesses can harness the benefits of cloud computing while minimizing security risks.

Regulatory compliance in cloud environments is a critical consideration for organizations operating in various industries.

Numerous laws, regulations, and industry standards govern the handling, storage, and transmission of data, and non-compliance can lead to severe legal and financial consequences.

Compliance requirements can vary widely based on factors such as geographic location, industry sector, and the type of data being processed.

For example, the European Union's General Data Protection Regulation (GDPR) places strict requirements on the handling of personal data, while the Health Insurance Portability and Accountability Act (HIPAA) in the United States regulates the protection of healthcare information.

Understanding and adhering to these regulations is essential for organizations, especially when considering the migration of data and workloads to cloud environments.

Cloud service providers often play a crucial role in helping organizations meet compliance requirements.

Many cloud providers offer services and features designed to simplify compliance, such as data encryption, access controls, and audit logs.

However, it's essential to recognize that compliance in the cloud is a shared responsibility between the cloud provider and the customer.

While cloud providers are responsible for securing the underlying infrastructure, customers are responsible for securing their data and applications within the cloud environment.

One of the primary challenges in cloud compliance is ensuring that the cloud provider's services align with the organization's specific compliance requirements.

To address this challenge, cloud providers undergo third-party audits and certifications to demonstrate their commitment to security and compliance.

Organizations should carefully review the compliance certifications held by their cloud providers and assess how they align with their industry and regulatory requirements.

Additionally, organizations must implement their own security controls and practices within the cloud environment to meet compliance obligations fully.

These controls may include role-based access control (RBAC), encryption, data loss prevention (DLP), and vulnerability assessments.

Organizations should also establish clear policies and procedures related to data handling, access management, and incident response.

Furthermore, data residency and cross-border data transfers are crucial aspects of compliance in cloud environments.

Many regulations require that certain types of data remain within specific geographic boundaries.

Cloud providers typically offer data center regions in various locations to accommodate these requirements, enabling organizations to store data in compliance with regional laws.

When considering cloud services, organizations should evaluate the provider's data center locations and ensure they align with their data residency needs.

Data encryption is a fundamental component of compliance in cloud environments.

Encryption helps protect data both at rest and in transit, safeguarding it from unauthorized access and breaches.

Organizations should implement encryption mechanisms that comply with relevant encryption standards and regulations.

Access controls are another critical aspect of compliance.

Role-based access control (RBAC) ensures that only authorized personnel can access sensitive data and resources within the cloud environment.

Organizations should regularly review and update access privileges to align with changing roles and responsibilities.

Regular monitoring and auditing are essential for demonstrating compliance and identifying potential security risks or breaches.

Many cloud providers offer built-in auditing and monitoring tools that can help organizations track access, changes, and security events within their cloud environment.

Organizations should configure these tools to generate audit logs that can be retained for compliance purposes.

When it comes to compliance documentation, organizations should maintain detailed records of their security practices, policies, and audit logs.

These records serve as evidence of compliance and can be invaluable in the event of an audit or investigation.

It's also essential to conduct regular compliance assessments and vulnerability scans within the cloud environment.

These assessments help identify and remediate security vulnerabilities and non-compliance issues promptly.

Ultimately, achieving and maintaining compliance in cloud environments is an ongoing effort that requires vigilance, a strong security posture, and a deep understanding of the regulatory landscape.

Collaboration between cloud providers, legal teams, compliance experts, and IT professionals is essential to navigate the complex web of regulations and ensure that organizations meet their compliance obligations.

In summary, regulatory compliance in cloud environments is a multifaceted challenge, but it is essential for organizations to operate within the bounds of the law and protect sensitive data.

By leveraging the tools and capabilities offered by cloud providers and implementing robust security practices, organizations can confidently embrace the cloud while meeting their compliance requirements.

Chapter 3: Understanding Cloud Service Models

Infrastructure as a Service (IaaS) is a fundamental cloud computing service model that provides organizations with virtualized computing resources over the internet.

At its core, IaaS delivers scalable and on-demand infrastructure components, such as virtual machines (VMs), storage, and networking, eliminating the need for organizations to purchase and maintain physical hardware.

This service model offers a flexible and cost-effective solution for businesses looking to deploy, manage, and scale their IT infrastructure.

In an IaaS environment, organizations can create and manage VMs, which serve as the building blocks of their computing resources.

These VMs can run various operating systems and applications, giving businesses the freedom to customize their computing environment to meet their specific needs.

IaaS providers typically offer a range of VM sizes and configurations, allowing organizations to choose resources that align with their performance and capacity requirements.

One of the key advantages of IaaS is its scalability.

Organizations can easily scale their infrastructure up or down based on changing demands, ensuring that they have the resources they need when they need them.

This elasticity is achieved through virtualization technology, which abstracts physical hardware resources into virtual instances.

IaaS providers manage the underlying physical infrastructure, including servers, storage, and networking equipment, ensuring that it is maintained, upgraded, and secured.

Customers, on the other hand, have control over the virtualized resources they provision and can manage them through web-based dashboards or APIs.

Storage is a critical component of IaaS, and providers offer various types of storage to cater to different use cases.

Block storage provides high-performance storage for VMs, while object storage is suitable for storing unstructured data like images, videos, and backups.

IaaS providers also offer file storage options for shared data between VMs.

Networking plays a crucial role in IaaS, allowing organizations to connect VMs, create virtual networks, and establish secure communication between resources.

IaaS providers typically offer a range of networking features, including load balancers, firewalls, and virtual private networks (VPNs).

One of the notable benefits of IaaS is cost efficiency.

Organizations no longer need to invest in and manage physical hardware, which can be capital-intensive and require ongoing maintenance.

Instead, they pay for IaaS resources on a pay-as-you-go or subscription basis, allowing them to align their infrastructure costs with their actual usage.

This cost model can result in significant savings, particularly for businesses with fluctuating computing needs.

IaaS also promotes business continuity and disaster recovery.

Data stored in the cloud can be replicated across multiple data centers, providing redundancy and minimizing the risk of data loss due to hardware failures or disasters.

In the event of a failure, applications and services can be quickly restored from backup instances.

Security is a paramount concern in IaaS environments.
Customers are responsible for securing their VMs and data within the cloud, while IaaS providers are responsible for securing the physical infrastructure and the virtualization layer.
Organizations must implement robust security measures, including access controls, encryption, and security patches, to protect their cloud resources.
Compliance with industry-specific regulations and data protection laws is another aspect of IaaS security.
Organizations must ensure that their cloud operations align with the necessary compliance requirements and standards.
To effectively manage IaaS resources, organizations can leverage automation and orchestration tools.
These tools enable the automation of routine tasks, such as provisioning and scaling, reducing manual overhead and enhancing operational efficiency.
IaaS providers typically offer a marketplace of pre-configured virtual machine images and services that can be easily deployed to meet specific business needs.
These images can include operating systems, applications, and development frameworks, allowing organizations to accelerate the deployment of new services and applications.
In summary, Infrastructure as a Service (IaaS) is a fundamental cloud computing service model that provides organizations with scalable and on-demand computing resources.
It offers cost efficiency, scalability, and flexibility, making it an attractive option for businesses of all sizes.
However, organizations must take responsibility for securing their resources within the cloud and ensure compliance with regulatory requirements.
By leveraging the capabilities of IaaS and implementing robust security practices, organizations can effectively

manage their IT infrastructure in the cloud and focus on their core business objectives.

Platform as a Service (PaaS) is a cloud computing service model that provides a comprehensive platform for developers to build, deploy, and manage applications without the complexities of managing underlying infrastructure.
PaaS is designed to streamline the application development process, allowing developers to focus on writing code and delivering innovative solutions rather than managing servers, storage, and networking.
In a PaaS environment, developers are provided with a set of tools, services, and frameworks that simplify application development and deployment.
This platform typically includes application development frameworks, database management systems, middleware, and integrated development environments (IDEs).
PaaS offers a range of benefits, including faster time-to-market for applications, improved collaboration among development teams, and enhanced scalability and flexibility.
Developers can access and utilize the platform's components and services through a web-based interface or application programming interfaces (APIs).
One of the key advantages of PaaS is its abstraction of infrastructure management.
Developers do not need to worry about server provisioning, hardware maintenance, or operating system updates.
Instead, they can focus on writing code and building applications that meet business needs.
PaaS providers handle the underlying infrastructure, ensuring that it is secure, scalable, and available.
This abstraction allows developers to work more efficiently and accelerates the development cycle.

PaaS platforms often support multiple programming languages, enabling developers to choose the language that best suits their project requirements.

This flexibility means that organizations can use PaaS for a wide range of application types, from web and mobile applications to data analytics and Internet of Things (IoT) solutions.

PaaS also promotes collaboration among development teams.

Multiple developers can work on the same project simultaneously, accessing and updating the application code and resources through the platform.

This collaboration leads to faster development cycles and improved productivity.

Furthermore, PaaS platforms typically offer built-in integration with other cloud services, such as databases, storage, and identity management.

This seamless integration simplifies the development process and allows developers to leverage additional cloud resources when needed.

Database management is a crucial component of PaaS.

PaaS providers offer various database services, including relational databases, NoSQL databases, and data warehousing solutions.

Developers can choose the database service that aligns with their application requirements and scale it as needed.

PaaS platforms also offer automated scaling, which allows applications to handle increased loads by automatically adding resources.

This scalability ensures that applications can handle varying levels of traffic and demand without manual intervention.

Security is a top priority in PaaS environments.

PaaS providers implement robust security measures, including data encryption, access controls, and identity management, to protect applications and data.

Customers are responsible for securing their application code and data within the PaaS platform.

Compliance with industry-specific regulations and data protection laws is essential when using PaaS for sensitive data and applications.

Developers can take advantage of the platform's monitoring and analytics tools to gain insights into application performance and user behavior.

These tools help identify and address performance bottlenecks and improve the overall user experience.

PaaS platforms often provide built-in support for continuous integration and continuous delivery (CI/CD) pipelines.

This support streamlines the deployment process, allowing developers to automate testing, deployment, and release cycles.

In summary, Platform as a Service (PaaS) is a cloud computing service model that empowers developers to build, deploy, and manage applications efficiently.

It abstracts the complexities of infrastructure management, promoting faster development, collaboration, and scalability.

PaaS platforms offer a wide range of tools and services to support various application types and programming languages. Security and compliance are paramount concerns, and developers must take responsibility for securing their application code and data within the PaaS environment. By leveraging the capabilities of PaaS and embracing modern development practices, organizations can accelerate their application development efforts and deliver innovative solutions to market.

Chapter 4: Cloud Security Fundamentals

The threat landscape in the cloud is dynamic and constantly evolving, presenting both challenges and opportunities for organizations.

As businesses increasingly migrate their data, applications, and workloads to cloud environments, they must also confront a wide range of security threats.

These threats span from traditional cyberattacks to cloud-specific vulnerabilities, and they require a proactive and comprehensive approach to mitigate.

One of the prominent threats in the cloud is unauthorized access, where malicious actors attempt to gain unauthorized entry to cloud resources, applications, or data.

These unauthorized access attempts can take the form of stolen credentials, phishing attacks, or exploiting misconfigured access controls.

To counter this threat, organizations should implement robust identity and access management (IAM) practices, including strong authentication and access monitoring.

Another significant concern is data breaches, which can have severe financial and reputational consequences.

Data breaches in the cloud can occur due to misconfigured storage, insecure APIs, or vulnerabilities in cloud-based applications.

To protect against data breaches, organizations should implement encryption, access controls, and regular security assessments.

Ransomware attacks are another growing threat in the cloud, where cybercriminals encrypt an organization's data and demand a ransom for its release.

Cloud-based backup and disaster recovery solutions are essential defenses against ransomware, allowing organizations to restore their data in case of an attack.

Distributed denial of service (DDoS) attacks remain a persistent threat in the cloud, disrupting services by overwhelming them with traffic.

Cloud providers often offer DDoS protection services, but organizations should also implement their own security measures, such as traffic filtering and rate limiting.

Misconfigurations are a common source of security vulnerabilities in the cloud.

These misconfigurations can result from human error, lack of awareness, or the complexity of cloud environments.

Organizations should regularly audit and review their cloud configurations to identify and rectify misconfigurations that could expose them to security risks.

Another emerging threat is supply chain attacks, where attackers compromise the software supply chain to distribute malicious code through trusted channels.

Organizations should implement strict software supply chain security practices and thoroughly vet third-party components used in their cloud applications.

Cloud-specific threats include serverless function attacks, where attackers exploit vulnerabilities in serverless code execution environments.

To mitigate this threat, organizations should follow secure coding practices and implement runtime security controls.

As organizations adopt containerization and orchestration technologies like Kubernetes, they must also be vigilant against container vulnerabilities and insecure configurations.

Regular security scanning and patching of container images and clusters are essential defenses.

API security is critical in the cloud, as APIs facilitate communication between cloud services and applications.

API vulnerabilities can lead to data exposure or unauthorized access.

Organizations should implement API security measures, including authentication, authorization, and rate limiting.

IoT devices and edge computing in the cloud introduce new security challenges.

Securing these devices and managing their data flows requires a comprehensive IoT security strategy.

Finally, the human element remains a significant factor in the cloud threat landscape.

Phishing attacks, social engineering, and insider threats pose risks to cloud security.

Employee training, awareness programs, and access controls can help mitigate these risks.

In summary, the threat landscape in the cloud is complex and multifaceted, requiring organizations to adopt a proactive and layered security approach.

Effective cloud security involves understanding the specific threats that exist in cloud environments, implementing robust security measures, and continuously monitoring and adapting to new threats.

By staying informed and taking a comprehensive approach to security, organizations can navigate the evolving cloud threat landscape and protect their valuable data and assets.

Security policies and procedures are essential components of any organization's cybersecurity strategy.

These policies and procedures provide a structured framework for safeguarding information, systems, and networks from security threats and vulnerabilities.

They serve as a guide for employees and stakeholders, outlining the rules and best practices for maintaining a secure computing environment.

Effective security policies and procedures address various aspects of security, from data protection to incident response and access control.

One of the foundational elements of security policies is data classification and handling.

Organizations should define how different types of data, such as sensitive customer information or proprietary business data, are classified and treated.

This classification helps determine the level of protection and access controls that should be applied to each category of data.

Access control policies and procedures dictate who has access to specific resources and under what circumstances.

They define user roles, privileges, and permissions, ensuring that only authorized individuals can access sensitive information and perform specific actions.

Password management policies and procedures are crucial for enforcing strong password practices.

These policies typically include rules for password complexity, expiration, and the prohibition of password sharing.

Multi-factor authentication (MFA) may also be mandated to add an extra layer of security.

Network security policies and procedures establish guidelines for securing an organization's network infrastructure.

They include measures such as firewall configuration, intrusion detection and prevention, and network segmentation to prevent unauthorized access and protect against cyber threats.

Incident response policies and procedures outline the steps to be taken in the event of a security incident or breach.

They detail how incidents should be reported, investigated, and mitigated to minimize damage and prevent future occurrences.

Security awareness and training policies and procedures ensure that employees are educated about security risks and best practices.

Regular training sessions and awareness programs help employees recognize phishing attempts, social engineering tactics, and other security threats.

Physical security policies and procedures extend security measures to the physical environment.

They address issues such as access to data centers, secure disposal of hardware, and visitor access to facilities.

Vendor management policies and procedures guide the assessment and monitoring of third-party vendors' security practices.

Organizations should ensure that their vendors meet specific security standards and compliance requirements to reduce supply chain risks.

Data retention and disposal policies specify how long different types of data should be retained and how they should be securely disposed of when no longer needed.

These policies help organizations comply with data privacy regulations and reduce the risk of data breaches.

Change management policies and procedures dictate how changes to the organization's IT environment are planned, tested, approved, and implemented.

This ensures that changes do not introduce security vulnerabilities or disrupt operations.

Remote access policies define the rules and requirements for employees and third parties accessing the organization's network and resources remotely.

They often include secure VPN connections, authentication, and monitoring of remote sessions.

Security policies and procedures should be reviewed and updated regularly to address new threats and technology changes.

An essential part of this process is conducting risk assessments to identify potential security gaps and vulnerabilities.

Employees and stakeholders must be made aware of any updates or changes to security policies and procedures through effective communication channels.

Additionally, organizations should establish a process for auditing and compliance checks to ensure that security policies are being followed and that the organization remains compliant with relevant regulations.

In summary, security policies and procedures are vital tools for organizations to protect their information and assets from security threats.

They provide clear guidelines and expectations for employees and stakeholders, helping to create a secure and resilient cybersecurity posture.

Chapter 5: Identity and Access Management

User authentication methods play a critical role in ensuring the security of digital systems and protecting sensitive information.

Authentication is the process of verifying the identity of a user, ensuring that the person or entity trying to access a system or application is indeed who they claim to be.

In the world of cybersecurity, user authentication is an essential step in the access control process, allowing organizations to grant or deny access to their resources based on the user's identity.

Traditionally, the most common form of user authentication is the use of usernames and passwords.

With this method, users provide a unique username and a corresponding password to gain access to a system or application.

The username identifies the user, while the password serves as the secret key that only the authorized user should know.

Despite its ubiquity, the username and password method has several limitations and security vulnerabilities.

Passwords can be weak, easily guessed, or stolen through various means, such as phishing attacks or data breaches.

To enhance security, organizations often require users to create complex passwords, which can be difficult to remember.

Furthermore, users may resort to reusing passwords across multiple accounts, increasing the risk of a breach in one account compromising others.

To address these limitations, many organizations have adopted multi-factor authentication (MFA) as a more secure authentication method.

MFA requires users to provide multiple forms of verification before granting access.

Typically, MFA combines something the user knows (password) with something the user has (a mobile device or smart card) and sometimes something the user is (biometric data like fingerprints or facial recognition).

This multi-layered approach significantly enhances security by adding an additional barrier for unauthorized access.

Biometric authentication methods use unique physical or behavioral characteristics to verify a user's identity.

These characteristics can include fingerprints, palm prints, facial features, iris scans, voice patterns, or even typing patterns.

Biometric authentication is highly secure since it is challenging for attackers to replicate or steal these biometric features.

It is also convenient for users as they don't need to remember passwords or carry physical tokens.

However, biometric data, once compromised, cannot be changed, and concerns about privacy and data protection have arisen in some cases.

Smart cards and tokens are physical devices that users carry to provide an additional authentication factor.

Smart cards contain embedded microprocessors and store cryptographic keys, while tokens generate one-time passwords or PINs.

To authenticate, users must insert the smart card or enter the token-generated code along with their password.

This method is particularly useful for securing remote access or highly sensitive systems.

However, users can lose these physical devices, and managing the distribution and replacement of tokens or cards can be administratively challenging.

Another authentication method gaining popularity is the use of mobile-based authentication apps.

These apps generate one-time passwords or push notifications to a user's mobile device, which the user then provides during login.

Mobile-based authentication is convenient as most users have smartphones, and the app can often be easily installed.

It also adds a layer of security since access requires both a password and physical possession of the mobile device.

However, users may still be vulnerable to mobile device theft or SIM card swapping attacks.

Contextual authentication is an adaptive approach that evaluates various factors, or context, surrounding a login attempt to determine its legitimacy.

Factors can include the user's location, the device they are using, their IP address, and their typical login behavior.

If the context aligns with the user's usual patterns, access is granted without requiring additional authentication.

However, if the context is unusual or suspicious, the system may trigger additional authentication steps.

This method helps balance security and usability, adapting authentication requirements based on the perceived risk.

Passwordless authentication is a modern approach that aims to eliminate the use of passwords altogether.

Instead, it relies on one or more alternative authentication methods, such as biometrics, smart cards, or mobile apps.

Users are authenticated without the need for a traditional password, reducing the risk associated with password-related vulnerabilities.

Passwordless authentication can enhance security and usability simultaneously.

However, its adoption may require organizations to invest in new infrastructure and user education.

Blockchain-based authentication methods are emerging as a novel approach to user authentication.

Blockchain technology creates a decentralized and tamper-resistant ledger of transactions or data.

In this context, blockchain can be used to verify user identities securely.

Users create digital identities stored on a blockchain, and these identities are verified through a consensus mechanism.

Once verified, users can use their blockchain-based identity to access various services securely.

Blockchain-based authentication can enhance security by reducing the risk of identity theft and data breaches.

However, it is still an evolving technology with scalability and regulatory challenges.

In summary, user authentication methods have evolved significantly to meet the growing demands of cybersecurity.

While traditional username and password authentication remains common, organizations increasingly turn to multi-factor authentication, biometrics, smart cards, and other innovative approaches to enhance security.

The choice of authentication method should align with an organization's security requirements, user experience goals, and technology infrastructure.

Role-Based Access Control (RBAC) is a crucial security model that helps organizations manage and control access to resources and data in the cloud.

RBAC allows organizations to define and enforce access permissions based on the roles and responsibilities of users within the organization.

This approach simplifies access management by grouping users with similar functions into roles and assigning permissions accordingly.

In RBAC, access permissions are typically predefined and associated with specific roles.

For example, an organization may define roles like "administrators," "developers," and "read-only users," each with different levels of access to resources.

Administrators may have full access, developers may have access to certain development environments, and read-only users may have access to view data without making changes.

RBAC ensures that users can only perform actions and access data that align with their job functions, reducing the risk of unauthorized access and data breaches.

Implementing RBAC in the cloud begins with defining roles and assigning permissions.

Organizations should carefully analyze their access needs and user responsibilities to create meaningful roles.

Once roles are defined, they can be associated with specific users or groups.

Cloud providers offer tools and dashboards that allow administrators to manage RBAC policies efficiently.

One of the key advantages of RBAC is its scalability.

As organizations grow and change, they can easily adapt RBAC policies to accommodate new roles and responsibilities.

This flexibility helps maintain a clear and consistent access control model, even in dynamic environments.

RBAC also simplifies user onboarding and offboarding.

When a new employee joins the organization, administrators can assign them to the appropriate role with predefined permissions.

Similarly, when an employee leaves, their access can be revoked by removing them from their role.

This process ensures that access is granted and revoked consistently and reduces the risk of orphaned accounts.

RBAC promotes the principle of least privilege (PoLP), which means users are granted the minimum level of access needed to perform their job functions.

By adhering to PoLP, organizations limit the potential damage that can result from a compromised account.

For example, if an attacker gains access to a user's account with limited privileges, they won't have the authority to perform critical actions or access sensitive data.

RBAC also helps organizations achieve compliance with regulatory requirements and industry standards.

Many regulations, such as the Health Insurance Portability and Accountability Act (HIPAA) and the General Data Protection Regulation (GDPR), require organizations to implement access controls and limit access to sensitive data.

RBAC provides a systematic way to meet these compliance requirements and demonstrate control over access.

It's important to periodically review and audit RBAC policies to ensure they remain aligned with the organization's needs and security posture.

Regular audits help identify and rectify any inconsistencies or deviations from the defined access controls.

Additionally, organizations should monitor user activities to detect any unusual or unauthorized access attempts.

Cloud providers often offer built-in monitoring and auditing tools that can assist in this regard.

While RBAC is a robust access control model, organizations should consider a few best practices to enhance its effectiveness.

First, organizations should document RBAC policies and make them easily accessible to all stakeholders.

Clear documentation helps users understand their access rights and responsibilities.

Second, organizations should provide training and awareness programs to educate users about RBAC and its importance in security.

Users should know how to request access changes and report any suspicious activity.

Lastly, RBAC should be part of a broader security strategy that includes other security measures such as encryption, authentication, and network security.

RBAC is most effective when combined with a comprehensive approach to security.

In summary, Role-Based Access Control (RBAC) is a vital component of cloud security that helps organizations manage and control access to resources and data based on users' roles and responsibilities.

RBAC simplifies access management, promotes the principle of least privilege, and enhances security by ensuring that users can only perform actions that align with their job functions.

By implementing RBAC and following best practices, organizations can achieve a more secure and compliant cloud environment.

Chapter 6: Data Security in the Cloud

Encryption is a fundamental technology that plays a critical role in protecting data privacy in today's digital age.

It involves the process of converting plaintext data into ciphertext, rendering it unreadable to anyone who does not possess the decryption key.

The primary goal of encryption is to ensure that even if unauthorized parties gain access to the encrypted data, they cannot understand or use it without the proper decryption key.

Encryption is used extensively to secure sensitive information, such as personal communication, financial transactions, and healthcare records, in various digital contexts.

There are two main types of encryption: symmetric and asymmetric encryption.

Symmetric encryption uses a single encryption key to both encrypt and decrypt data.

This key must be kept confidential and shared securely between the sender and the recipient.

Symmetric encryption is efficient and fast, making it suitable for encrypting large volumes of data, but it poses a challenge in securely exchanging the encryption key.

Asymmetric encryption, on the other hand, uses a pair of keys: a public key for encryption and a private key for decryption.

The public key can be freely shared, allowing anyone to encrypt data that only the holder of the corresponding private key can decrypt.

This approach eliminates the need for secure key exchange but is computationally more intensive and slower than symmetric encryption.

Data privacy is a fundamental concept in the digital world, emphasizing the rights and control that individuals have over their personal information.

Protecting data privacy means safeguarding sensitive data from unauthorized access, disclosure, alteration, or destruction.

Data breaches, identity theft, and privacy violations have highlighted the critical importance of data privacy in the digital era.

Encryption serves as a powerful tool to enhance data privacy by ensuring that even if data is intercepted or stolen, it remains inaccessible without the proper decryption key.

One of the most common applications of encryption for data privacy is secure communication.

When you send an email, engage in online banking, or access a secure website, encryption is often used to protect the confidentiality of the data transmitted between your device and the server.

Transport Layer Security (TLS) and its predecessor, Secure Sockets Layer (SSL), are widely used cryptographic protocols that establish secure communication channels over the internet.

They encrypt data during transmission, preventing eavesdroppers from intercepting and understanding the information.

Similarly, Virtual Private Networks (VPNs) employ encryption to create secure tunnels over public networks, ensuring the privacy of data traffic.

Another critical aspect of data privacy is data at rest, which refers to data that is stored on devices, servers, or in the cloud.

Encryption techniques like full-disk encryption (FDE) and file-level encryption protect data at rest by ensuring that even if an unauthorized person gains access to the storage medium, they cannot read the encrypted data without the decryption key.

Modern operating systems often offer built-in tools for enabling full-disk encryption, making it accessible to a broader range of users.

Data privacy regulations and laws, such as the European Union's General Data Protection Regulation (GDPR) and the California Consumer Privacy Act (CCPA), have placed greater emphasis on protecting individuals' personal information.

These regulations require organizations to implement robust data protection measures, which often include encryption, to safeguard sensitive data and maintain compliance.

Data breaches have far-reaching consequences, including reputational damage, financial losses, and legal liabilities, making data privacy a top priority for organizations and individuals alike.

In addition to secure communication and data at rest, encryption also plays a vital role in securing data in transit.

This includes encrypting data as it moves within and between cloud services, as well as within data centers.

Cloud providers offer encryption services and features to ensure that data remains confidential and protected throughout its journey.

End-to-end encryption is a particularly strong form of encryption that ensures data remains encrypted from the sender to the recipient, with no intermediate parties having access to the plaintext data.

End-to-end encryption is commonly used in secure messaging apps, where only the sender and recipient hold the encryption keys.

While encryption is a powerful tool for data privacy, it is not without challenges and considerations.

One challenge is key management, as securely storing and managing encryption keys is crucial to the overall security of encrypted data.

Lost or compromised keys can lead to data loss or unauthorized access.

Another consideration is the potential impact of encryption on system performance, as cryptographic operations can be computationally intensive.

Organizations must strike a balance between security and usability when implementing encryption.

Additionally, encryption alone does not guarantee data privacy; access controls, secure practices, and compliance with data protection regulations are equally important.

In summary, encryption is a fundamental technology that enhances data privacy by protecting data from unauthorized access and ensuring its confidentiality.

It is widely used in secure communication, data at rest, and data in transit to safeguard sensitive information in various digital contexts.

While encryption is a powerful tool, it should be part of a broader data protection strategy that includes key management, access controls, and compliance with data privacy regulations.

Data loss prevention (DLP) strategies are a crucial component of any organization's data security efforts, aimed at preventing the accidental or intentional exposure of sensitive data.

DLP strategies encompass a range of techniques and tools designed to identify, monitor, and protect sensitive information from unauthorized access or disclosure.

The first step in creating a DLP strategy is to understand what constitutes sensitive data within an organization.

Sensitive data can include personally identifiable information (PII), financial records, intellectual property, healthcare data, and more.

Identifying and classifying sensitive data is essential for determining how it should be protected.

Once sensitive data is identified, organizations can implement access controls and encryption to safeguard it.

Access controls restrict who can access sensitive data, ensuring that only authorized individuals or systems can view or modify it.

Encryption protects data by transforming it into an unreadable format that can only be decrypted with the appropriate encryption key.

Data discovery and classification tools play a vital role in identifying sensitive data within an organization's vast data repositories.

These tools scan data sources to identify and classify sensitive information based on predefined criteria, such as credit card numbers, social security numbers, or proprietary documents.

By automating this process, organizations can gain insight into where sensitive data resides and take appropriate protective measures.

Endpoint DLP solutions focus on securing data on individual devices, such as laptops, smartphones, and tablets.

These solutions often include features like content inspection, which scans data on endpoints for sensitive information, and encryption, which encrypts data on the device.

Endpoint DLP helps protect data even when it's accessed and stored on mobile devices outside the corporate network.

Network DLP solutions monitor data as it moves across the network, identifying and preventing unauthorized data transfers or leaks.

These solutions can inspect network traffic, email attachments, and file transfers to ensure that sensitive data does not leave the organization without proper authorization.

Cloud DLP extends data protection to cloud environments and cloud-based services.

As organizations increasingly store data in the cloud, it's essential to implement DLP controls that can monitor and protect data in cloud storage and collaboration platforms.

Cloud DLP solutions integrate with cloud services to enforce policies and prevent data breaches.

Content discovery and monitoring are critical capabilities of DLP solutions.

These features enable organizations to scan and analyze content within files, emails, and other communication channels to identify and prevent the sharing of sensitive data.

Content monitoring can include the detection of specific keywords, patterns, or file types that are indicative of sensitive information.

Policy enforcement is a fundamental aspect of DLP strategies.

Organizations must define clear DLP policies that dictate how sensitive data should be handled, shared, and protected.

These policies should align with regulatory requirements and industry standards.

Policy enforcement mechanisms ensure that employees and systems adhere to these guidelines, preventing unauthorized data exposure.

User education and awareness are essential elements of DLP strategies.

Employees should be trained on data security best practices, including recognizing and handling sensitive data appropriately.

Security awareness programs help create a culture of data protection within the organization.

Regularly updating and fine-tuning DLP policies and rules is crucial to adapt to evolving threats and changing business requirements.

Periodic reviews and assessments of DLP configurations and policies help ensure that the organization remains protected against new risks.

Incident response and reporting are critical components of DLP strategies.

In the event of a DLP incident or breach, organizations need a well-defined incident response plan to contain and mitigate the damage.

Additionally, reporting mechanisms should be in place to provide insights into DLP incidents, trends, and areas of concern.

Data loss prevention strategies should also consider insider threats, which can pose a significant risk to sensitive data.

Insiders, whether intentionally or unintentionally, can expose sensitive data.

Monitoring user activity and behavior, as well as implementing user-based policies and controls, can help detect and prevent insider threats.

Regularly auditing and analyzing DLP logs and events can provide valuable insights into potential vulnerabilities and risks.

Organizations should use DLP logs to track policy violations, monitor user behavior, and identify emerging threats.

Integrating DLP solutions with other security tools, such as SIEM (Security Information and Event Management) systems, enhances overall data protection capabilities.

By sharing DLP data with broader security systems, organizations can correlate information and respond more effectively to security incidents.

In summary, data loss prevention (DLP) strategies are essential for safeguarding sensitive data in organizations.

These strategies encompass a range of techniques and tools, including data discovery, access controls, encryption, and content monitoring, to prevent unauthorized access or exposure of sensitive information.

A comprehensive DLP strategy should align with regulatory requirements, include user education, and regularly adapt to emerging threats and changing business needs.

Chapter 7: Network Security in Cloud Environments

Virtual Private Cloud (VPC) security is a fundamental aspect of cloud computing, as VPCs are a critical component that allows organizations to create isolated and secure network environments within a public cloud infrastructure.

A VPC is a virtual network that provides a private and isolated network space within a cloud provider's data centers.

It allows organizations to segment their cloud resources logically, ensuring that their workloads and data remain separate and protected from other users in the same cloud environment.

VPCs are the foundation upon which organizations build their cloud infrastructure, making VPC security paramount.

One of the primary security considerations for VPCs is network isolation, which ensures that resources within a VPC can only communicate with each other and are shielded from the public internet.

This isolation is achieved through network access control lists (ACLs) and security groups that define the allowed traffic flow within the VPC.

Network ACLs act as a firewall at the subnet level, controlling inbound and outbound traffic based on rules defined by the organization.

Security groups, on the other hand, are associated with individual resources, such as instances, and control traffic at a more granular level.

Organizations should configure network ACLs and security groups carefully to restrict traffic to only necessary communication, reducing the attack surface.

Another critical aspect of VPC security is secure network architecture.

Organizations should design their VPCs with security in mind, adhering to best practices for network segmentation, subnet design, and routing.

For example, placing resources with different security requirements into separate subnets can help limit access and reduce the impact of potential breaches.

Properly configuring route tables within the VPC ensures that traffic is directed correctly and securely.

Data encryption is a fundamental security measure in VPCs.

Organizations should implement encryption for data both in transit and at rest.

For data in transit, the use of Virtual Private Network (VPN) connections or direct connections to the cloud provider's network ensures encrypted communication between on-premises data centers and the VPC.

Additionally, using Transport Layer Security (TLS) for communication between services and endpoints within the VPC adds an extra layer of encryption.

Encrypting data at rest means using encryption mechanisms to protect data stored in cloud resources like Elastic Block Store (EBS) volumes and Amazon S3 buckets.

Cloud providers offer encryption options that organizations can enable to protect their data.

Identity and access management (IAM) plays a crucial role in VPC security.

Organizations should implement strong IAM policies to control who can access and manage VPC resources.

IAM policies should follow the principle of least privilege (PoLP), ensuring that users and applications have only the permissions they need to perform their tasks.

Regularly auditing and reviewing IAM policies helps maintain their accuracy and effectiveness.

Monitoring and logging are essential components of VPC security.

Cloud providers offer tools and services for monitoring VPC activity, such as Amazon CloudWatch and Azure Monitor.

These tools can detect and alert organizations to suspicious activities or potential security incidents.

Additionally, organizations should enable logging for VPC resources and review log data regularly to identify security events or policy violations.

Security automation and orchestration are becoming increasingly important in VPC security.

Organizations should leverage automation tools to enforce security policies consistently and respond to security incidents in real time.

For example, auto-scaling groups can automatically add or remove instances based on demand while adhering to security group rules.

DevOps practices can also help automate security checks and tests during the development and deployment of cloud resources.

Multi-factor authentication (MFA) should be enforced for accessing VPC management consoles and critical systems.

MFA adds an extra layer of security by requiring users to provide two or more authentication factors, such as a password and a temporary code sent to their mobile device.

This additional authentication step helps prevent unauthorized access to VPC resources.

Regular security assessments, vulnerability scans, and penetration tests should be conducted to identify and address security weaknesses in the VPC.

These assessments can help organizations proactively detect and remediate vulnerabilities before they are exploited by attackers.

Organizations should also stay informed about the latest security threats and best practices in VPC security.

Cloud providers continually update their security features and services, and organizations should take advantage of these enhancements to strengthen VPC security.

In summary, Virtual Private Cloud (VPC) security is a critical aspect of cloud computing that organizations must prioritize to protect their cloud resources and data.

By implementing network isolation, secure architecture, encryption, strong identity and access controls, monitoring, automation, and other security measures, organizations can create a robust and resilient VPC security strategy that defends against evolving cyber threats.

Intrusion Detection and Prevention Systems (IDPS) are vital components of a modern cybersecurity strategy, designed to detect and respond to unauthorized or malicious activities within computer systems and networks.

These systems are a critical layer of defense against cyber threats, providing organizations with real-time monitoring and protection against a wide range of cyberattacks.

The primary function of an IDPS is to identify suspicious or anomalous behavior that could indicate a security breach or an impending attack.

To achieve this, IDPS solutions rely on a variety of techniques, including signature-based detection, anomaly-based detection, and behavioral analysis.

Signature-based detection involves comparing network traffic or system activity to known attack patterns or signatures.

When a match is found, the IDPS generates an alert, allowing security personnel to investigate and respond to the threat.

Anomaly-based detection, on the other hand, focuses on identifying deviations from established baselines of normal behavior.

The IDPS continuously monitors network traffic or system activity and raises alerts when it detects activities that do not align with established norms.

Behavioral analysis takes a broader view by looking at the overall behavior of users and systems within the network.

It seeks to identify unusual patterns or trends that may indicate malicious activities, even if those activities do not match known attack signatures.

IDPS solutions can be categorized into two main types: network-based and host-based.

Network-based IDPS monitors network traffic and activities at the network perimeter, between network segments, or within a specific network zone.

It examines packets of data as they traverse the network and analyzes them for signs of intrusion or malicious behavior.

Host-based IDPS, on the other hand, focuses on individual hosts or devices within a network.

It monitors the activities and processes occurring on a specific system, looking for indications of compromise or unauthorized access.

Both network-based and host-based IDPS solutions have their strengths and are often used in conjunction to provide comprehensive protection.

One of the key advantages of IDPS solutions is their ability to provide real-time threat detection and immediate alerts.

When suspicious activity is detected, the IDPS can generate alerts or trigger automated responses, allowing security teams to react swiftly and mitigate potential threats before they escalate.

IDPS solutions also contribute to incident response efforts by providing valuable information about the nature of the threat, its source, and its impact on the network or system.

This information is essential for understanding and containing the incident effectively.

To enhance their effectiveness, IDPS solutions often incorporate machine learning and artificial intelligence (AI) algorithms.

These technologies enable the IDPS to continuously learn and adapt to evolving threats, improving detection accuracy and reducing false positives.

Machine learning models can analyze vast amounts of data to identify subtle patterns and anomalies that might go unnoticed by traditional rule-based systems.

Furthermore, IDPS solutions can be integrated with other security tools and systems, such as Security Information and Event Management (SIEM) platforms and firewall appliances.

This integration allows organizations to correlate IDPS alerts with other security events and data sources, providing a more comprehensive view of the threat landscape.

It also streamlines incident response efforts by centralizing security information and enabling automated responses to certain threats.

However, while IDPS solutions offer many benefits, they also present some challenges.

One of the primary challenges is the potential for false positives and false negatives.

False positives occur when the IDPS generates alerts for legitimate activities mistaken as suspicious.

False negatives, on the other hand, happen when the IDPS fails to detect actual threats.

Balancing the sensitivity of the IDPS to reduce false negatives while minimizing false positives is a continuous challenge for security teams.

Another challenge is the constant evolution of cyber threats.

As attackers become more sophisticated, they employ tactics designed to evade detection by traditional IDPS solutions.

This necessitates ongoing updates and enhancements to IDPS capabilities to keep pace with emerging threats.

Moreover, IDPS solutions can generate a significant volume of alerts and data, which can overwhelm security teams.

Effective management of these alerts and efficient incident response processes are essential for maximizing the value of IDPS investments.

Intrusion Detection and Prevention Systems are subject to various deployment options, including inline and out-of-band configurations.

Inline IDPS solutions actively inspect and filter network traffic in real time, blocking or allowing traffic based on detected threats.

Out-of-band IDPS solutions, on the other hand, analyze a copy of network traffic or logs, allowing for a more passive approach to threat detection.

The choice between inline and out-of-band deployment depends on an organization's specific security requirements and network architecture.

In summary, Intrusion Detection and Prevention Systems (IDPS) are essential tools in the arsenal of cybersecurity defenses.

They play a critical role in identifying and responding to unauthorized or malicious activities within computer systems and networks.

IDPS solutions use a variety of techniques, including signature-based detection, anomaly-based detection, and behavioral analysis, to detect and mitigate threats.

They provide real-time threat detection, immediate alerts, and contribute to incident response efforts.

While IDPS solutions offer significant benefits, they also come with challenges, including the potential for false positives and the need to keep up with evolving threats.

Effective IDPS deployment, management, and integration with other security tools are key to maximizing their effectiveness in protecting organizations from cyber threats.

Chapter 8: Compliance and Governance in the Cloud

Cloud compliance frameworks are essential tools for organizations operating in the cloud, providing a structured approach to ensuring adherence to regulatory requirements, industry standards, and best practices.

These frameworks serve as guidelines and reference models that help organizations implement and maintain robust compliance programs in their cloud environments.

One of the primary challenges organizations face when adopting cloud services is understanding and managing compliance responsibilities.

Cloud providers typically operate under a shared responsibility model, where they are responsible for the security of the cloud infrastructure, while customers are responsible for securing their data and applications within the cloud.

Compliance frameworks help organizations navigate this shared responsibility model by providing clarity on the specific compliance controls they need to address.

These frameworks cover a wide range of compliance domains, including data protection, identity and access management, encryption, and audit logging.

By adopting a compliance framework, organizations can streamline their compliance efforts, reduce the risk of regulatory violations, and demonstrate their commitment to data security and privacy.

One of the most widely recognized cloud compliance frameworks is the Cloud Security Alliance (CSA) Cloud Controls Matrix (CCM).

The CCM is a comprehensive set of cloud-specific security controls aligned with various industry standards and best practices.

It provides organizations with a structured approach to assessing and managing security and compliance risks in the cloud.

The CCM covers a broad range of topics, including governance, risk management, data protection, and security operations.

Another notable compliance framework is the National Institute of Standards and Technology (NIST) Cybersecurity Framework.

While not specific to the cloud, the NIST framework provides a valuable reference for organizations looking to enhance their cybersecurity posture in the cloud.

It focuses on five core functions: identify, protect, detect, respond, and recover, and offers guidelines for implementing security controls to achieve these functions.

The NIST framework is widely adopted and recognized as a valuable resource for cloud security and compliance.

For organizations subject to specific regulatory requirements, industry-specific compliance frameworks may be more relevant.

For example, healthcare organizations often adhere to the Health Insurance Portability and Accountability Act (HIPAA) and can use the NIST framework in conjunction with HIPAA-specific guidance for cloud compliance.

Similarly, financial institutions may need to comply with the Payment Card Industry Data Security Standard (PCI DSS) and can leverage the PCI DSS requirements tailored to cloud environments.

The European Union's General Data Protection Regulation (GDPR) is another significant regulatory framework that organizations worldwide must consider when storing or processing EU residents' personal data in the cloud.

Compliance frameworks provide organizations with a structured approach to assess their cloud security posture and identify areas for improvement.

They offer a clear set of controls and best practices that organizations can use to evaluate their compliance with specific requirements.

Organizations can use compliance frameworks to conduct self-assessments, gap analyses, and audits to ensure that their cloud environments align with industry standards and regulatory requirements.

Furthermore, compliance frameworks help organizations prepare for external audits or assessments by providing a structured framework that auditors can use to evaluate compliance.

Cloud compliance frameworks are not static; they evolve to address new challenges and emerging threats in the cloud landscape.

As cloud technology advances, compliance frameworks are updated to include relevant controls and recommendations.

Organizations should stay informed about updates to these frameworks to ensure that their cloud environments remain compliant and secure.

In addition to providing guidelines for compliance, many frameworks offer practical recommendations and best practices for cloud security.

These recommendations cover a wide range of topics, including data encryption, access control, security monitoring, and incident response.

By following these best practices, organizations can enhance their cloud security posture and reduce the risk of data breaches and security incidents.

Furthermore, compliance frameworks often include guidance on risk management, helping organizations identify, assess, and mitigate risks associated with their cloud deployments.

Organizations can use risk assessments based on these frameworks to prioritize security investments and allocate resources effectively.

Implementing a cloud compliance framework is not a one-time effort but an ongoing process.

Organizations must continually monitor and assess their cloud environments to ensure that they remain compliant with regulatory requirements and industry standards.

Regular audits and assessments help organizations identify and address compliance gaps and vulnerabilities.

Additionally, organizations should stay informed about changes to relevant regulations and standards that may impact their compliance obligations.

In summary, cloud compliance frameworks are invaluable tools for organizations seeking to navigate the complex landscape of cloud security and compliance.

These frameworks provide structured guidance and best practices to help organizations assess and manage compliance risks in the cloud.

By adopting and implementing compliance frameworks, organizations can strengthen their cloud security posture, reduce the risk of data breaches, and demonstrate their commitment to data security and privacy.

Auditing and reporting are fundamental components of compliance efforts for organizations across various industries and sectors.

They play a critical role in ensuring that organizations adhere to regulatory requirements, industry standards, and internal policies.

Auditing involves the systematic examination and evaluation of an organization's processes, controls, and activities to assess compliance and identify areas of improvement.

The objective of auditing is to provide assurance that the organization is operating in accordance with established rules and guidelines.

Compliance auditing is particularly essential in industries where data security, privacy, and regulatory adherence are paramount, such as healthcare, finance, and information technology.

Auditors, whether internal or external, assess an organization's policies, procedures, and practices to determine whether they meet compliance requirements.

They review documentation, interview employees, and perform testing to validate that controls are in place and effective.

One of the most common types of compliance audits is the financial audit, which focuses on an organization's financial statements and transactions.

Financial audits are typically conducted by external auditors to ensure the accuracy and completeness of financial reporting.

They assess the organization's financial controls, transactions, and records to identify any discrepancies or irregularities.

Operational audits, on the other hand, examine an organization's operational processes and procedures.

These audits assess whether the organization's operations are efficient, effective, and compliant with internal policies and industry regulations.

Operational audits aim to identify opportunities for improvement in processes, resource utilization, and risk management.

In the context of compliance, regulatory audits are conducted to assess an organization's adherence to specific laws and regulations.

For example, in the healthcare industry, organizations may undergo Health Insurance Portability and Accountability Act (HIPAA) audits to ensure compliance with patient data protection requirements.

Similarly, financial institutions may be subject to audits related to the Payment Card Industry Data Security Standard (PCI DSS) or the Sarbanes-Oxley Act (SOX).

Compliance audits can also focus on information security and data protection.

In an era of increasing cyber threats and data breaches, information security audits have become crucial.

These audits evaluate an organization's information security policies, controls, and practices to ensure that data is protected from unauthorized access, disclosure, or alteration.

Information security audits often include assessments of network security, data encryption, access controls, and incident response plans.

Another important aspect of auditing for compliance is vendor or third-party audits.

Organizations often rely on third-party vendors or service providers for various functions, including cloud hosting, payment processing, and data storage.

Vendor audits assess the third party's compliance with contractual obligations, security standards, and data protection requirements.

Organizations must ensure that their vendors meet the same level of compliance to safeguard their data and operations.

Internal audits, conducted by an organization's internal audit team, provide a proactive approach to compliance.

Internal auditors assess an organization's operations, controls, and policies to identify potential compliance issues and recommend improvements.

Internal audits help organizations stay ahead of compliance requirements and address issues before external audits or regulatory agencies become involved.

Auditing for compliance generates a wealth of data and information.

Reporting is the process of documenting audit findings, conclusions, and recommendations in a clear and comprehensive manner.

Effective reporting is essential for communication between auditors and organizational stakeholders, including management, board members, and regulatory authorities.

Audit reports typically include details about the scope of the audit, the audit methodology, findings, conclusions, and recommendations.

They may also include evidence gathered during the audit, such as documentation, interviews, and test results.

Audit reports are valuable tools for decision-making and accountability.

They provide organizations with insights into their compliance status, potential risks, and areas for improvement.

Management relies on audit reports to make informed decisions about process enhancements, risk mitigation, and resource allocation.

Audit reports also serve as a historical record of compliance efforts, which can be useful for demonstrating adherence to regulatory requirements in case of audits or investigations.

Furthermore, audit reports may include management responses or action plans to address audit findings.

These responses outline the steps management intends to take to remediate identified issues and improve compliance.

Management responses demonstrate a commitment to addressing compliance concerns and ensuring continuous improvement.

Transparency is a key principle of effective auditing and reporting for compliance.

Organizations should be open and transparent about their audit processes, findings, and remediation efforts.

This transparency builds trust with stakeholders, including customers, investors, and regulatory authorities.

Regular communication about audit activities and compliance status helps foster a culture of compliance within an organization.

Auditing and reporting for compliance are not one-time events but ongoing processes.

Organizations must establish a regular audit schedule to ensure that they continuously monitor and assess their compliance efforts.

Regular audits help organizations identify evolving risks, adapt to changes in regulations, and address emerging threats. Furthermore, organizations should engage in continuous improvement by incorporating lessons learned from audits into their compliance programs.

In summary, auditing and reporting for compliance are essential components of an organization's efforts to meet regulatory requirements, industry standards, and internal policies. Auditing provides an objective assessment of an organization's compliance status, while reporting communicates findings, conclusions, and recommendations to stakeholders.

Effective auditing and reporting promote transparency, accountability, and a culture of compliance within an organization, ultimately safeguarding its reputation and operations.

Chapter 9: Security Best Practices for Azure, AWS, and GCP

Azure, Microsoft's cloud computing platform, offers a wide range of services and features to help organizations build, deploy, and manage their applications and data securely in the cloud.

As organizations increasingly rely on Azure for their business-critical workloads, it becomes imperative to follow Azure security best practices to protect their assets and maintain a strong security posture.

One of the fundamental principles of Azure security is the shared responsibility model, which outlines the division of security responsibilities between Microsoft as the cloud provider and the customer.

Under this model, Microsoft is responsible for the security of the cloud infrastructure, including the physical data centers, networking, and the underlying hardware and software.

On the other hand, the customer is responsible for securing their data, applications, identities, and access management within Azure.

To secure their Azure resources, organizations should implement strong identity and access management practices.

Azure Active Directory (Azure AD) is a central component for managing identities and access to Azure services.

Organizations should enforce multi-factor authentication (MFA) for user accounts to add an additional layer of security.

Role-Based Access Control (RBAC) is another critical aspect of identity and access management in Azure.

RBAC enables organizations to grant permissions to users and groups based on their roles and responsibilities, ensuring that users have only the necessary access to perform their tasks.

Azure provides a range of security tools and services to help organizations protect their cloud resources.

Azure Security Center is a central hub for monitoring and managing the security of Azure deployments.

It provides recommendations for improving security, threat detection, and incident response capabilities.

Organizations should regularly review and act upon the recommendations provided by Azure Security Center to strengthen their security posture.

For securing virtual machines (VMs) in Azure, organizations should leverage Azure Disk Encryption to protect data at rest.

Azure Disk Encryption uses BitLocker for Windows VMs and DM-Crypt for Linux VMs to encrypt the OS and data disks.

This ensures that even if a VM's underlying storage is compromised, the data remains encrypted.

Network security is a critical consideration in Azure.

Organizations should use Azure Network Security Groups (NSGs) to control inbound and outbound traffic to their resources.

NSGs act as virtual firewalls and allow organizations to define rules that permit or deny traffic based on source IP, destination IP, port, and protocol.

Implementing Azure DDoS Protection is another essential step to safeguard against distributed denial-of-service (DDoS) attacks.

Azure DDoS Protection automatically detects and mitigates DDoS attacks, ensuring that services remain available during an attack.

Organizations should also monitor network traffic and application behavior using Azure Monitor and Azure Application Insights.

These tools provide insights into the performance and security of Azure resources, helping organizations detect and respond to suspicious activities.

Data security is a top priority in Azure.

Organizations should use Azure Key Vault to manage and safeguard cryptographic keys and secrets used by their applications and services.

Key Vault provides hardware security modules (HSMs) to protect keys and enforce access policies.

Additionally, Azure provides data encryption capabilities, including Azure SQL Database Transparent Data Encryption (TDE) and Azure Storage Service Encryption (SSE).

These features ensure that data is encrypted both at rest and in transit.

Azure also offers Azure Information Protection, which enables organizations to classify and label sensitive data, apply protection policies, and track data usage.

For securing containerized applications in Azure Kubernetes Service (AKS), organizations should follow best practices for container security.

This includes regularly patching and updating container images, limiting container privileges, and scanning container images for vulnerabilities.

Azure Policy is a valuable tool for enforcing compliance with organizational standards and best practices.

Organizations can use Azure Policy to define and enforce policies that govern the configuration of Azure resources.

These policies help ensure that resources are deployed and configured securely and in compliance with regulatory requirements.

In addition to these technical security measures, organizations should establish an incident response plan for Azure.

An incident response plan outlines the procedures to follow in the event of a security incident, including detection, containment, eradication, and recovery.

Regular training and drills are essential to ensure that the incident response team is prepared to respond effectively to security incidents.

Azure security best practices also extend to compliance with regulatory standards and certifications.

Azure complies with a wide range of industry standards and regulatory frameworks, including ISO 27001, HIPAA, and GDPR.

Organizations should assess their specific compliance requirements and leverage Azure's compliance offerings to ensure that their deployments align with these standards.

In summary, Azure security best practices are essential for organizations to protect their assets and data in the Azure cloud.

By following these best practices for identity and access management, network security, data security, and compliance, organizations can build and maintain a robust security posture in Azure.

Regular monitoring, threat detection, and incident response planning are crucial components of a comprehensive Azure security strategy, helping organizations safeguard their cloud resources and data effectively.

AWS (Amazon Web Services) is a leading cloud service provider that offers a vast array of services and features to help organizations build and manage their applications and data in the cloud securely.

As more organizations migrate their workloads to AWS, it becomes essential to follow AWS security best practices to protect their assets and maintain a strong security posture.

One of the foundational principles of AWS security is the shared responsibility model, which outlines the division of security responsibilities between AWS as the cloud provider and the customer.

Under this model, AWS is responsible for the security of the cloud infrastructure, including the physical data centers, networking, and the underlying hardware and software.

The customer, on the other hand, is responsible for securing their data, applications, identities, and access management within AWS.

Identity and access management are critical components of AWS security.

AWS Identity and Access Management (IAM) is a central service that helps organizations manage user identities, roles, and permissions.

To enhance security, organizations should implement strong authentication practices, such as multi-factor authentication (MFA), for their AWS IAM users.

Role-Based Access Control (RBAC) in IAM allows organizations to assign specific permissions to users and resources based on their roles, helping ensure that users have only the necessary access to perform their tasks.

Securing data in AWS is paramount, and AWS provides a range of services and features to help organizations achieve this.

For data at rest, organizations should use Amazon S3 (Simple Storage Service) server-side encryption to encrypt their data.

AWS Key Management Service (KMS) allows organizations to manage encryption keys securely and define access policies for these keys.

For data in transit, organizations should enable SSL/TLS (Secure Sockets Layer/Transport Layer Security) encryption for data transferred between AWS services and clients.

Network security is another crucial aspect of AWS security.

Amazon Virtual Private Cloud (VPC) enables organizations to isolate their AWS resources in a private network and control inbound and outbound traffic using Network Access Control Lists (NACLs) and Security Groups.

AWS Web Application Firewall (WAF) protects web applications from common web exploits and attacks.

AWS Shield provides protection against distributed denial-of-service (DDoS) attacks, ensuring the availability of AWS resources during an attack.

Monitoring and logging are essential for detecting and responding to security incidents in AWS.

AWS CloudTrail records API calls and activities in an AWS account, providing an audit trail for actions taken.

AWS Config enables organizations to assess, audit, and evaluate the configurations of their AWS resources.

Amazon CloudWatch allows organizations to monitor and collect logs, metrics, and events from AWS resources and applications.

Additionally, AWS GuardDuty is a managed threat detection service that continuously monitors for malicious activity and unauthorized behavior in AWS accounts.

For securing AWS EC2 (Elastic Compute Cloud) instances, organizations should regularly patch and update their instances with the latest security patches.

AWS Systems Manager provides tools for managing and automating updates across a fleet of EC2 instances. AWS also offers AWS Inspector, a security assessment service that helps organizations identify security vulnerabilities in their EC2 instances.

Container security is crucial for organizations using AWS Elastic Container Service (ECS) or Amazon Elastic Kubernetes Service (EKS).

Best practices include scanning container images for vulnerabilities, limiting container privileges, and implementing network segmentation for containers.

AWS security best practices extend to compliance with regulatory standards and certifications.

AWS complies with a wide range of industry standards and regulatory frameworks, such as ISO 27001, HIPAA, and PCI DSS.

Organizations should assess their specific compliance requirements and leverage AWS's compliance offerings and resources to ensure their AWS deployments align with these standards.

Incident response planning is a vital aspect of AWS security.

Organizations should establish an incident response plan that outlines the procedures to follow in the event of a security incident, from detection to resolution.

Regular training and tabletop exercises help ensure that the incident response team is well-prepared to respond effectively to security incidents.

In summary, AWS security best practices are essential for organizations to protect their assets and data in the AWS cloud.

By following these best practices for identity and access management, data security, network security, monitoring, and compliance, organizations can build and maintain a robust security posture in AWS.

Regular monitoring, threat detection, and incident response planning are crucial components of a comprehensive AWS security strategy, helping organizations safeguard their cloud resources and data effectively.

Chapter 10: Cloud Security Tools and Resources

Cloud security assessment tools are invaluable resources for organizations seeking to evaluate and enhance the security of their cloud environments.

In an era of increasing reliance on cloud services and the growing sophistication of cyber threats, these tools play a critical role in helping organizations identify vulnerabilities, assess risks, and ensure compliance with security best practices.

These tools are designed to provide organizations with insights into their cloud security posture by analyzing configurations, monitoring for security threats, and conducting vulnerability assessments.

One of the primary functions of cloud security assessment tools is to perform cloud configuration assessments.

These assessments involve evaluating the settings and configurations of cloud resources and services to ensure they align with security best practices and compliance requirements.

For example, a configuration assessment tool may check whether encryption is enabled for data storage, whether access controls are correctly configured, and whether firewall rules are properly defined.

By identifying misconfigurations and deviations from best practices, organizations can proactively address potential security risks.

Another crucial aspect of cloud security assessment tools is continuous monitoring.

These tools continuously monitor cloud environments for security threats and suspicious activities, providing real-time alerts and insights into potential security incidents.

They can detect activities such as unauthorized access, unusual login patterns, and data exfiltration attempts.

By monitoring cloud environments 24/7, organizations can respond promptly to security incidents and minimize the impact of breaches.

Vulnerability assessments are also a core function of cloud security assessment tools.

These assessments involve scanning cloud resources and services for known vulnerabilities and weaknesses.

Vulnerability assessment tools check for outdated software, missing security patches, and misconfigured settings that could be exploited by attackers.

By identifying vulnerabilities, organizations can prioritize remediation efforts to reduce the attack surface and enhance security.

Furthermore, cloud security assessment tools often offer compliance assessment capabilities.

These capabilities help organizations ensure that their cloud environments adhere to regulatory standards and industry-specific compliance requirements.

For example, healthcare organizations must comply with the Health Insurance Portability and Accountability Act (HIPAA), while financial institutions may need to adhere to the Payment Card Industry Data Security Standard (PCI DSS).

Compliance assessment tools check whether cloud configurations and practices align with these standards and provide recommendations for compliance.

Cloud security assessment tools come in various forms, including Software as a Service (SaaS) solutions, on-premises solutions, and cloud-native offerings.

SaaS-based tools are hosted in the cloud and require minimal setup and maintenance, making them accessible to organizations of all sizes.

On-premises solutions are installed and operated within an organization's own infrastructure, offering complete control but requiring more management.

Cloud-native offerings are specifically designed for cloud environments, leveraging cloud-native APIs and integrations for seamless security assessments.

Many cloud service providers offer their own cloud security assessment tools and services.

For example, AWS provides AWS Security Hub, a comprehensive security service that aggregates security findings from multiple AWS services and third-party solutions.

Azure offers Azure Security Center, which provides advanced threat protection across Azure resources and hybrid workloads.

Google Cloud offers Google Cloud Security Command Center, a security and data risk platform that provides visibility and insights into cloud assets and data.

Additionally, there are numerous third-party cloud security assessment tools available in the market, each with its own unique features and capabilities.

The choice of a cloud security assessment tool depends on an organization's specific needs, cloud provider, and budget.

When selecting a tool, organizations should consider factors such as the depth of assessment, ease of integration with existing systems, scalability, and the quality of reporting and alerts.

Integration with existing security tools and workflows is crucial for streamlining security operations and incident response.

Furthermore, organizations should ensure that the chosen tool supports the cloud environments and services they use, whether it's AWS, Azure, Google Cloud, or a multi-cloud environment.

Ultimately, cloud security assessment tools are essential components of a comprehensive cloud security strategy.

They provide organizations with the visibility, insights, and automation needed to assess and improve their cloud security posture continuously.

By using these tools, organizations can proactively identify and mitigate security risks, enhance compliance, and protect their cloud resources and data from evolving threats.

In summary, cloud security assessment tools are indispensable assets for organizations operating in the cloud.

They help organizations assess and enhance their cloud security posture by conducting configuration assessments, continuous monitoring, vulnerability assessments, and compliance checks.

Choosing the right tool that aligns with an organization's specific needs and cloud environment is crucial for effective cloud security management.

The cloud security community and forums serve as vibrant hubs of knowledge exchange and collaboration for professionals and enthusiasts alike in the ever-evolving field of cloud security.

These digital spaces provide valuable opportunities for individuals to connect, share insights, seek guidance, and stay updated on the latest developments in cloud security.

One of the primary benefits of participating in a cloud security community or forum is the access to a diverse pool of expertise and experience.

Members of these communities come from various backgrounds, ranging from seasoned cybersecurity experts to beginners looking to expand their knowledge.

This diversity fosters a rich environment for learning and networking, where individuals can tap into the collective wisdom of the community.

For those new to cloud security, these forums offer a supportive environment where they can ask questions and seek guidance from more experienced members.

Experienced professionals, in turn, have the opportunity to mentor and share their knowledge, contributing to the growth of the next generation of cloud security practitioners.

Cloud security communities and forums often host discussions on a wide range of topics relevant to cloud security.

These topics may include best practices for securing cloud environments, strategies for mitigating emerging threats, and insights into compliance and regulatory requirements.

Participants can engage in discussions, ask questions, and share their own experiences and solutions.

This collaborative approach to problem-solving is invaluable in an industry where threats and technologies are constantly evolving.

Members of these communities often share real-world anecdotes and case studies, illustrating how they tackled specific cloud security challenges.

These stories provide practical insights and lessons learned that can help others navigate similar situations.

Additionally, cloud security communities frequently feature experts and thought leaders who share their expertise through webinars, articles, and presentations.

These resources offer valuable educational opportunities and help members stay informed about the latest trends and innovations in cloud security.

Participating in a cloud security community or forum can also lead to professional growth and career development.

Members can showcase their expertise, establish themselves as subject matter experts, and build their professional networks.

Engagement in these communities can open doors to collaboration, job opportunities, and speaking engagements at industry events.

Furthermore, many cloud security communities and forums offer certifications and training programs to help individuals enhance their skills and credentials.

These certifications can be a valuable addition to a professional's resume and serve as proof of their expertise in cloud security.

Beyond individual benefits, cloud security communities and forums also contribute to the advancement of the field as a whole.

Members often collaborate on research projects, contribute to open-source security tools, and publish whitepapers and reports on relevant topics.

This collective effort helps drive innovation and knowledge dissemination, ultimately raising the overall level of cloud security expertise in the industry.

While the benefits of cloud security communities and forums are numerous, it's essential to approach participation with certain considerations in mind.

Firstly, individuals should be mindful of the security and privacy of the information they share.

While these communities are generally safe spaces for professionals to discuss security matters, it's crucial not to disclose sensitive or confidential information.

Additionally, participants should adhere to community guidelines and codes of conduct, promoting respectful and constructive interactions.

As with any online platform, there may be differences of opinion and occasional disagreements.

However, it's important to maintain a professional and courteous tone in discussions, focusing on the exchange of ideas rather than engaging in confrontations.

When seeking guidance or advice, it's helpful to provide context and details about specific challenges or scenarios to receive more tailored responses.

This allows community members to offer more precise guidance and solutions.

Furthermore, individuals should take advantage of the search functionality within these communities to explore existing discussions and find answers to common questions.

Many questions have likely been addressed in previous threads, saving time and effort.

It's also beneficial to follow experts and thought leaders within the community to stay updated on their contributions and insights.

In summary, cloud security communities and forums play a pivotal role in fostering collaboration, knowledge sharing, and professional growth within the field of cloud security.

These digital spaces offer a wealth of resources, from educational content to real-world experiences and expert insights.

Participation in these communities not only benefits individuals but also contributes to the collective advancement of cloud security as a discipline.

By engaging respectfully, adhering to best practices, and embracing the opportunity for continuous learning, individuals can maximize the benefits of these invaluable platforms.

BOOK 2
MASTERING CLOUD SECURITY
ADVANCED STRATEGIES FOR AZURE, AWS, AND GCP

ROB BOTWRIGHT

Chapter 1: Advanced Cloud Security Landscape

The landscape of threats in the cloud is continually evolving, presenting a dynamic challenge for organizations that rely on cloud services to conduct their business.

As technology advances and the adoption of cloud computing continues to grow, threat actors adapt and refine their tactics to exploit vulnerabilities in cloud environments.

Understanding the nature of evolving threats in the cloud is essential for organizations to build effective security strategies and protect their data and applications.

One of the most prominent threats in the cloud is data breaches, which occur when unauthorized parties gain access to sensitive data stored in cloud repositories.

These breaches can result from a variety of factors, including misconfigured access controls, weak authentication, or compromised credentials.

Threat actors often target cloud storage services, such as Amazon S3 buckets or Azure Blob Storage, where organizations store vast amounts of data.

Ransomware attacks have also evolved to target cloud environments, encrypting data and demanding a ransom for decryption keys.

To counter these threats, organizations must implement robust access controls, encryption, and multi-factor authentication to safeguard their data.

Another evolving threat in the cloud is the rise of sophisticated phishing attacks targeting cloud-based email services.

Phishing emails that lure users into providing their credentials can lead to unauthorized access to email accounts and sensitive information.

Attackers use social engineering techniques to craft convincing emails that appear legitimate, making it challenging for users to discern the phishing attempts.

Organizations should educate their employees about recognizing phishing attempts and deploy email security solutions that can detect and block such attacks.

Cloud-native applications and microservices have introduced a new set of security challenges.

As organizations adopt containerization and serverless computing, they must consider the security of the underlying infrastructure and the code they deploy.

Vulnerabilities in container images, for example, can be exploited to compromise the entire containerized application.

Security scanning of container images and continuous monitoring of containerized workloads are essential measures to address these evolving threats.

Serverless functions, while providing scalability and flexibility, can also be vulnerable to attacks.

Organizations should implement security best practices for serverless computing, including runtime monitoring and access control.

Misconfiguration of cloud resources remains a persistent threat in the cloud.

As organizations deploy a wide range of cloud services and resources, errors in configuration can inadvertently expose sensitive data or grant unauthorized access.

Security groups, network access controls, and identity and access management policies must be configured correctly to prevent these types of threats.

Cloud service providers regularly update their services and introduce new features, but these updates can also introduce vulnerabilities if not properly managed.

Patch management and timely application of security updates are crucial to mitigate these risks.

Supply chain attacks, where attackers compromise software components or dependencies, have also become a growing concern in the cloud.

Threat actors may target open-source libraries or third-party components used in cloud applications.

Organizations should maintain visibility into their software supply chain, conduct security assessments, and monitor for vulnerabilities in dependencies.

In the cloud, shared responsibility for security between the cloud provider and the customer introduces complexities in threat management.

While cloud providers secure the infrastructure, customers are responsible for securing their data, applications, and configurations.

This shared responsibility requires a clear understanding of each party's obligations and a proactive approach to security.

Additionally, insider threats remain a challenge in the cloud.

Employees or contractors with access to cloud resources can intentionally or unintentionally compromise security.

Implementing strong identity and access management controls and monitoring user activities can help detect and prevent insider threats.

Security automation and orchestration have become critical tools in addressing evolving threats in the cloud.

Automated responses to security events, such as the isolation of compromised resources or the deployment of security patches, can significantly reduce response times.

Many cloud providers offer security automation features and integrations with security orchestration platforms.

Machine learning and artificial intelligence technologies are also playing a growing role in cloud security.

These technologies can analyze vast amounts of data to detect anomalies and potential security threats.

Machine learning models can help identify suspicious activities or patterns in cloud environments, enabling proactive threat detection.

As organizations embrace multi-cloud and hybrid cloud architectures, managing security across diverse environments becomes more complex.

Evolving threats can target specific cloud providers or exploit vulnerabilities in the connections between on-premises and cloud resources.

Organizations must adopt a holistic approach to security that spans all cloud environments, on-premises infrastructure, and network connections.

Cybersecurity threats in the cloud are not limited to technology alone; they also involve regulatory and compliance considerations.

Organizations must navigate the complex landscape of data protection laws and compliance requirements relevant to their industry and geographical location.

Failure to meet these obligations can result in legal consequences and reputational damage.

In summary, evolving threats in the cloud demand continuous vigilance and proactive security measures from organizations.

Data breaches, phishing attacks, misconfigurations, supply chain vulnerabilities, and insider threats are just a few examples of the multifaceted challenges organizations face in the cloud.

By staying informed about emerging threats, implementing robust security practices, and leveraging automation and AI-driven solutions, organizations can effectively mitigate the risks and ensure the security of their cloud environments.

Cloud security is a dynamic field that constantly evolves in response to emerging trends and evolving challenges in the digital landscape.

Staying ahead of these trends and addressing the associated challenges is crucial for organizations seeking to protect their data, applications, and infrastructure in the cloud.

One of the prominent trends in cloud security is the increasing adoption of cloud-native technologies.

Organizations are leveraging containers, serverless computing, and microservices to build scalable and agile applications.

While these technologies offer many benefits, they also introduce new security considerations.

Securing containerized applications, for example, requires vulnerability scanning and runtime monitoring to detect and address security issues.

Serverless functions, on the other hand, require robust access controls and monitoring to prevent unauthorized access.

Another significant trend is the growing complexity of multi-cloud and hybrid cloud environments.

Many organizations use multiple cloud providers or combine on-premises infrastructure with cloud resources to meet their business needs.

Managing security across these diverse environments presents challenges in terms of consistency and visibility.

Each cloud provider has its own security tools and services, making it essential for organizations to adopt a unified security strategy that spans all cloud environments.

The proliferation of data and the increasing reliance on cloud storage services have also led to data security becoming a top concern.

Data breaches and unauthorized access incidents can have severe consequences for organizations, including financial losses and reputational damage.

Encrypting data both at rest and in transit is critical, and organizations must implement robust access controls and monitoring to safeguard sensitive information.

Phishing attacks targeting cloud-based email services have become more sophisticated, with attackers using social engineering tactics to deceive users.

These attacks can result in compromised accounts and unauthorized access to sensitive data.

Educating employees about recognizing phishing attempts and implementing email security measures are essential steps to mitigate this threat.

In the cloud, misconfigurations remain a persistent security challenge.

Misconfigured cloud resources can inadvertently expose data or grant unauthorized access.

Security groups, network access controls, and identity and access management policies must be configured correctly to prevent these issues.

Supply chain attacks, where attackers compromise software components or dependencies, have gained prominence.

Attackers may target open-source libraries or third-party components used in cloud applications.

Organizations should maintain visibility into their software supply chain, conduct security assessments, and monitor for vulnerabilities in dependencies.

The shared responsibility model of cloud security, which divides responsibilities between the cloud provider and the customer, can sometimes lead to confusion and potential gaps in security.

Organizations must have a clear understanding of their responsibilities and take proactive measures to secure their data and applications.

Insider threats in the cloud are another concern.

Employees or contractors with access to cloud resources can intentionally or unintentionally compromise security.

Implementing strong identity and access management controls and monitoring user activities are essential for detecting and preventing insider threats.

Security automation and orchestration have become vital tools in addressing cloud security challenges.

Automated responses to security events, such as isolating compromised resources or deploying security patches, can significantly reduce response times.

Many cloud providers offer security automation features and integrations with security orchestration platforms.

Machine learning and artificial intelligence (AI) technologies are increasingly applied in cloud security.

These technologies can analyze vast amounts of data to detect anomalies and potential threats.

Machine learning models can help identify suspicious activities or patterns in cloud environments, enabling proactive threat detection.

Compliance with regulatory requirements and data protection laws is an ongoing challenge for organizations operating in the cloud.

Different regions and industries have varying compliance obligations that organizations must meet.

Failure to comply can result in legal consequences and reputational damage.

Hybrid work models and remote work trends have accelerated the adoption of cloud-based collaboration and communication tools.

While these tools offer convenience, they also introduce security risks, as sensitive information may be shared and accessed from various locations and devices.

Securing these tools and educating users about best practices are essential for protecting data and communications.

Lastly, the evolving threat landscape necessitates continuous monitoring and threat intelligence sharing.

Organizations must keep abreast of emerging threats and vulnerabilities and collaborate with the broader security community to stay informed.

Sharing threat intelligence can help organizations proactively defend against evolving threats.

In summary, cloud security trends and challenges are ever-present as technology evolves and threat actors adapt.

To navigate this dynamic landscape, organizations must remain vigilant, educate their staff, implement robust security practices, and leverage automation and AI-driven solutions.

Addressing these challenges is an ongoing process that requires a proactive and adaptable approach to cloud security.

Chapter 2: Secure Design and Architecture in the Cloud

Cloud security by design principles are foundational guidelines that organizations should embrace to build robust and effective security into their cloud environments from the ground up.

These principles enable organizations to proactively address security challenges and threats, reducing vulnerabilities and ensuring the protection of sensitive data and critical resources.

The first principle of cloud security by design is the principle of least privilege.

This principle emphasizes the importance of granting users and applications only the minimum level of access necessary to perform their tasks.

By limiting access to the bare essentials, organizations can reduce the risk of unauthorized actions and data breaches.

The principle of defense in depth is another crucial aspect of cloud security.

It involves implementing multiple layers of security controls and measures to create a comprehensive security posture.

This multi-layered approach ensures that even if one layer is breached, other layers provide additional protection.

Encryption is a fundamental principle in cloud security by design.

Data should be encrypted both at rest and in transit to protect it from unauthorized access.

Encryption algorithms and key management practices should be carefully selected and implemented to maintain the confidentiality and integrity of data.

Identity and access management (IAM) is a core principle that revolves around managing user identities and controlling their access to cloud resources.

Organizations should adopt strong IAM practices, such as multi-factor authentication (MFA) and role-based access control (RBAC), to enforce strict access control.

Automation is a key enabler of cloud security by design.

Automated security processes, including security orchestration and response, can help organizations respond swiftly to threats and vulnerabilities.

Automated security scans and compliance checks also aid in identifying and addressing security issues.

Visibility and monitoring are essential principles in cloud security.

Organizations should maintain visibility into their cloud environments through continuous monitoring and auditing.

This helps in detecting and responding to security incidents and identifying suspicious activities.

Compliance is a critical consideration in cloud security by design.

Organizations must adhere to regulatory standards and industry-specific compliance requirements.

Cloud security measures should be aligned with these standards to ensure legal and regulatory compliance.

Security awareness and training for employees are fundamental principles in cloud security.

Educating staff about security best practices and the risks associated with cloud computing helps create a security-conscious workforce.

Secure development practices are essential for building secure cloud applications and services.

Developers should follow secure coding standards, conduct regular security testing, and address vulnerabilities early in the development lifecycle.

The principle of data classification and labeling emphasizes the importance of categorizing data based on its sensitivity.

By classifying data and applying appropriate labels, organizations can ensure that sensitive information is adequately protected.

Secure networking is a crucial aspect of cloud security by design.

Organizations should implement network security controls, such as firewalls, intrusion detection systems, and virtual private networks (VPNs), to protect data in transit.

Resilience and disaster recovery principles are essential to ensure business continuity.

Organizations should have robust backup and recovery strategies in place to mitigate the impact of unexpected disruptions or data loss.

Cloud providers often offer tools and services to support these principles.

Third-party security assessments and audits are vital to validate the effectiveness of cloud security measures.

Organizations should engage independent assessors to evaluate their cloud security posture and identify areas for improvement.

Incident response and incident management are key principles in cloud security.

Organizations should have well-defined incident response plans in place to handle security incidents effectively.

These plans should include communication strategies, escalation procedures, and recovery steps.

The principle of continuous improvement underscores the need for ongoing assessment and enhancement of cloud security.

Organizations should regularly review and update their security measures to adapt to evolving threats and technologies.

Collaboration with the security community is a principle that encourages organizations to share threat intelligence and best practices.

Participating in industry groups and information-sharing initiatives can enhance the collective security posture.

Lastly, accountability is a central principle in cloud security by design.

Organizations should establish clear lines of responsibility for security and designate individuals or teams to oversee and enforce security policies and practices.

In summary, cloud security by design principles are essential guidelines that organizations should embrace to build a secure and resilient cloud environment.

These principles encompass a wide range of considerations, from access control and encryption to incident response and continuous improvement.

By incorporating these principles into their cloud security strategy, organizations can reduce risks and ensure the protection of their data and assets in the cloud.

Cloud architecture best practices are foundational guidelines and principles that organizations should follow when designing and deploying cloud-based solutions to achieve efficiency, scalability, reliability, and security.

These practices are essential for harnessing the full potential of cloud computing and ensuring that cloud environments meet business needs effectively.

One of the key cloud architecture best practices is to adopt a modular and decoupled architecture.

This approach involves breaking down complex systems into smaller, independent modules or microservices that can be developed, deployed, and scaled independently.

Modularity and decoupling enable flexibility, making it easier to update and maintain cloud applications.

Another essential best practice is to leverage cloud-native services and technologies.

Cloud providers offer a wide array of native services for various purposes, such as computing, storage, databases, and AI/ML.

By using these services, organizations can reduce operational overhead, improve scalability, and take advantage of built-in security features.

Scalability is a core consideration in cloud architecture.

Designing applications to be horizontally scalable means that they can handle increased workloads by adding more instances or resources.

This flexibility allows organizations to respond to changing demand effectively.

High availability and fault tolerance are critical best practices for ensuring that cloud applications are resilient to failures.

Redundancy, load balancing, and automatic failover mechanisms should be incorporated into the architecture to minimize downtime.

Security is a paramount concern in cloud architecture.

Implementing security best practices, such as network segmentation, encryption, and identity and access management, is crucial to protect data and resources.

Security should be considered from the initial design phase and throughout the entire lifecycle of cloud applications.

Cost optimization is an ongoing best practice for cloud architecture.

Cloud resources can become expensive if not managed effectively.

Organizations should regularly monitor and optimize resource usage to control costs.

Automation is a key enabler of cloud architecture best practices.

Automating tasks like provisioning, scaling, and monitoring helps reduce manual intervention, lowers the risk of human errors, and improves efficiency.

Organizations should use infrastructure as code (IaC) to automate resource provisioning and management.

Monitoring and observability are essential best practices for gaining insights into the performance and health of cloud applications.

Implementing monitoring tools and practices allows organizations to detect issues early and make informed decisions.

Compliance and governance are vital considerations in cloud architecture.

Organizations must adhere to regulatory requirements and internal policies.

Implementing automated compliance checks and audits helps ensure that cloud environments remain compliant.

A well-defined disaster recovery and backup strategy is another best practice.

Organizations should regularly back up data and have a plan in place to recover quickly from unexpected disruptions or data loss.

Cloud architecture should be designed to be vendor-agnostic when possible.

Avoiding cloud provider lock-in enables organizations to switch providers or adopt a multi-cloud strategy more easily. Flexibility and portability are key benefits of this approach.

Consideration of data locality and data residency is essential, especially in global organizations.

Understanding where data is stored and ensuring it complies with regional data privacy regulations is crucial.

Efficient data storage and management are best practices for optimizing cloud costs.

Choosing the appropriate storage options, such as object storage, block storage, or database services, based on the specific use case can result in significant cost savings.

Application performance optimization is an ongoing best practice.

Fine-tuning applications for cloud environments, optimizing code, and minimizing latency contribute to better performance.

Network design and architecture are critical considerations in cloud deployments.

Implementing robust networking, including virtual private clouds (VPCs), subnets, and security groups, helps secure and isolate resources effectively.

Caching and content delivery are best practices for improving the speed and responsiveness of cloud applications.

Content delivery networks (CDNs) and caching mechanisms help reduce latency and enhance the user experience.

Resource tagging is a best practice for managing and tracking cloud resources effectively.

Tagging resources with metadata allows organizations to categorize, search, and organize resources efficiently.

Application modernization is a consideration for organizations with legacy applications.

Modernizing applications by refactoring or rearchitecting them for the cloud can lead to improved scalability and cost-efficiency.

Cloud governance and cost management practices should involve cost allocation and budgeting.

Organizations should allocate costs to different departments or teams and set budgets to control spending.

Integration with existing on-premises systems is a best practice for organizations with hybrid cloud environments.

Ensuring seamless communication between on-premises and cloud resources is crucial for data exchange and business continuity.

Lastly, documentation and knowledge sharing are essential best practices for ensuring that cloud architecture and processes are well-documented and accessible to all relevant teams.

This documentation aids troubleshooting, onboarding, and maintaining compliance.

In summary, cloud architecture best practices encompass a wide range of considerations, from modularity and scalability to security, cost optimization, and documentation.

By following these best practices, organizations can build efficient, resilient, and secure cloud environments that meet their business objectives effectively.

Chapter 3: Advanced Identity and Access Management

Federated identity and Single Sign-On (SSO) are fundamental concepts in the realm of identity and access management (IAM) that streamline and enhance the user authentication experience across multiple applications and systems.

In today's digital landscape, where individuals often need to access a multitude of online services and applications, the ability to manage identities efficiently and securely is paramount.

Federated identity, in essence, is a way to establish a user's identity across multiple domains or organizations without requiring them to have separate usernames and passwords for each.

Consider a scenario where a user needs access to various services provided by different organizations, such as email, cloud storage, and online banking.

Without federated identity, the user would typically have to maintain separate credentials for each service, leading to password fatigue and increased security risks.

However, with federated identity, a user can log in once, and that authentication carries over to other services seamlessly.

The core principle behind federated identity is the concept of trust between different domains or organizations.

In a federated identity model, a trusted entity, often referred to as an Identity Provider (IdP), vouches for the user's identity.

When the user attempts to access a service, the service provider (SP) trusts the IdP's assertion and grants access without requiring the user to re-enter their credentials.

This trust relationship simplifies the user experience while maintaining a high level of security.

Single Sign-On (SSO) is a crucial component of federated identity.

It allows users to authenticate themselves once and gain access to multiple applications or services without needing to log in separately for each.

SSO eliminates the need for users to remember numerous usernames and passwords, reducing the likelihood of weak passwords or password reuse.

The benefits of SSO extend beyond user convenience.

It also enhances security by centralizing authentication and enabling organizations to implement robust security measures in a single location—the Identity Provider.

To illustrate the concept of federated identity and SSO further, let's consider a practical example.

Imagine a large corporation that uses various cloud-based services, such as email, document collaboration, and customer relationship management (CRM) tools.

Without SSO and federated identity, employees would need to log in separately to each of these services.

This would not only be time-consuming but could also result in security vulnerabilities if employees choose weak passwords or write them down.

By implementing federated identity and SSO, the corporation can set up a centralized Identity Provider (IdP), such as Active Directory Federation Services (ADFS) or a cloud-based IdP service.

When employees log in to their workstations or a company portal, they authenticate themselves with the IdP using their corporate credentials.

Once authenticated, the IdP issues a token or assertion that represents the user's identity.

Now, when an employee accesses any cloud-based service within the organization, the service trusts the IdP's assertion, granting access without requiring the user to re-enter their credentials.

This not only simplifies the user experience but also provides a centralized point for enforcing security policies and monitoring user activity.

Federated identity and SSO also play a crucial role in enhancing security beyond the corporate environment.

In the world of online services, users are accustomed to signing in with their Google, Facebook, or other social media accounts.

These social media platforms often act as Identity Providers, allowing users to access various third-party services without creating new accounts.

For example, a user can log in to a travel booking website using their Google credentials.

This integration simplifies the user experience and increases user engagement on third-party websites.

However, it's essential to note that while federated identity and SSO offer numerous benefits, they also introduce security considerations.

A compromised IdP can potentially grant unauthorized access to multiple services, making the IdP a valuable target for attackers.

Therefore, organizations must implement robust security measures to protect the Identity Provider.

Multi-factor authentication (MFA) is often recommended to add an extra layer of security to the authentication process.

Additionally, auditing and monitoring tools are essential to detect and respond to any suspicious activities within the federated identity environment.

In summary, federated identity and Single Sign-On (SSO) are powerful concepts that streamline user authentication and access to multiple services while maintaining security.

These mechanisms simplify the user experience, reduce the risk of password-related security incidents, and enhance overall security by centralizing authentication and enforcing security policies.

As organizations and online services continue to adopt federated identity and SSO, it is essential to strike a balance between usability and security, implementing best practices to protect both users and the Identity Provider.

Multifactor Authentication (MFA) is a critical security strategy designed to enhance the protection of user accounts and sensitive data by requiring multiple forms of verification before granting access.

In the modern digital landscape, where cyber threats continue to evolve, relying solely on a username and password for authentication is no longer sufficient to safeguard against unauthorized access.

MFA introduces an additional layer of security, making it significantly more challenging for attackers to compromise user accounts.

At its core, MFA relies on the principle of "something you know, something you have, and something you are."

These three factors encompass different types of authentication methods that can be combined to provide a higher level of assurance about the user's identity.

The "something you know" factor typically refers to traditional knowledge-based authentication, such as a password or a personal identification number (PIN).

While passwords have been the standard for decades, they have notable weaknesses.

Users often select weak passwords or reuse them across multiple accounts, making it easier for attackers to gain unauthorized access.

To strengthen this factor, organizations should encourage users to create strong, unique passwords and consider the use of passphrase-based authentication, which involves longer, more complex phrases.

Additionally, implementing policies that enforce password changes and discourage password reuse can further enhance security.

The "something you have" factor introduces an element of possession-based authentication.

This factor relies on the user having a physical token or device that generates or receives authentication codes.

One common implementation of this factor is a one-time password (OTP) generated by a hardware or software token.

Users typically receive these OTPs through a dedicated token device or a mobile app.

OTP-based MFA adds an extra layer of security because even if an attacker has the user's password, they would also need access to the physical token or device to gain entry.

Furthermore, time-based OTPs provide an additional layer of security by expiring after a short period, making them less susceptible to replay attacks.

Biometric authentication, such as fingerprint or facial recognition, represents the "something you are" factor.

Biometrics are unique physical or behavioral characteristics that can be used to verify an individual's identity.

These characteristics include fingerprint patterns, facial features, iris scans, and even voiceprints.

Biometric authentication has become increasingly popular due to its convenience and effectiveness.

Mobile devices and laptops often incorporate biometric sensors, allowing users to unlock their devices or authenticate transactions using their fingerprints or faces.

Biometric data is challenging to replicate, making it a robust authentication factor.

However, it's crucial to secure biometric data properly to prevent potential breaches.

Combining these authentication factors creates a multifaceted security strategy.

For example, a common MFA implementation involves combining something the user knows (a password) with something the user has (a mobile app generating OTPs).

When the user attempts to access a system or application, they enter their password (something they know).

Simultaneously, the MFA system sends an OTP to their mobile app (something they have).

To complete the authentication process, the user enters the OTP from their app, thus proving their identity through both knowledge and possession factors.

MFA strategies can vary in complexity and sophistication.

For instance, organizations can implement MFA on a per-user basis or apply it selectively to specific applications or systems based on the level of sensitivity or risk associated with the accessed resources.

Moreover, some MFA solutions offer adaptive authentication, which assesses the risk level of a login attempt and adjusts the authentication requirements accordingly.

For instance, if a user attempts to access a system from an unrecognized device or location, the MFA system may prompt for additional authentication factors, such as a fingerprint scan or a security question.

Authentication methods are not one-size-fits-all; they should align with the organization's security policies and the specific use cases.

While MFA significantly enhances security, it's essential to strike a balance between security and usability.

Overly complex MFA processes can frustrate users and lead to lower adoption rates.

Organizations should carefully consider user experience when implementing MFA, striving for a seamless and user-friendly authentication process.

Furthermore, MFA is not a one-time setup; it requires ongoing management and monitoring.

Organizations should have mechanisms in place to handle lost or compromised tokens or devices and to reset MFA settings when necessary.

Additionally, robust logging and auditing practices should be implemented to track authentication attempts and identify any suspicious activities.

In summary, multifactor authentication (MFA) is a crucial security strategy that enhances protection against unauthorized access by requiring multiple forms of verification before granting entry.

MFA combines knowledge-based authentication (something you know), possession-based authentication (something you have), and biometric authentication (something you are) to create a robust and layered approach to identity verification.

When implementing MFA, organizations should consider the balance between security and usability, select appropriate authentication methods, and ensure proper management and monitoring to maintain a secure environment.

Chapter 4: Encryption and Key Management

Advanced encryption algorithms are at the forefront of modern information security, playing a pivotal role in safeguarding sensitive data across a wide range of applications and communication channels.

As digital technology continues to advance, the need for robust encryption becomes increasingly critical to protect data from unauthorized access and interception.

One of the fundamental concepts in encryption is the transformation of plaintext, which is readable and understandable data, into ciphertext, which is scrambled and unintelligible to anyone without the decryption key.

This transformation ensures that even if malicious actors intercept the ciphertext, they cannot decipher it without the appropriate decryption key.

Advanced encryption algorithms are designed to provide a high level of security against various attack methods, including brute force attacks, which involve trying every possible key until the correct one is found.

Modern encryption algorithms employ complex mathematical operations and are resistant to such attacks, making them a vital component of data protection.

One of the most well-known and widely used encryption algorithms is the Advanced Encryption Standard (AES).

AES is a symmetric-key encryption algorithm, meaning the same key is used for both encryption and decryption.

It operates on blocks of data and supports key lengths of 128, 192, or 256 bits.

AES has become the de facto standard for securing data in a wide range of applications, from securing data at rest in databases to encrypting data in transit over networks.

The strength of AES lies in its ability to provide a high level of security while maintaining efficiency in terms of computational resources.

Another significant encryption algorithm is RSA (Rivest-Shamir-Adleman), which is asymmetric-key encryption.

RSA uses a pair of keys: a public key for encryption and a private key for decryption.

The security of RSA is based on the mathematical difficulty of factoring the product of two large prime numbers, which forms the public key.

As long as the prime factors remain secret, it is computationally infeasible for attackers to determine the private key.

RSA is often used for securing communications and digital signatures, and it plays a crucial role in securing online transactions and web communication through the use of SSL/TLS protocols.

While symmetric and asymmetric encryption algorithms are essential components of modern security, they are not the only ones.

Hash functions are cryptographic algorithms that take an input (or "message") and produce a fixed-size string of characters, which is typically a hexadecimal number.

The output, known as the hash value or digest, is unique to the input data, and even a small change in the input data results in a significantly different hash value.

Hash functions serve various purposes in cryptography, one of which is data integrity verification.

By comparing the hash value of received data with the expected hash value, users can detect whether the data has been tampered with during transmission.

Commonly used hash functions include MD5, SHA-1, and SHA-256.

However, due to vulnerabilities and advances in computing power, MD5 and SHA-1 are no longer considered secure for critical applications.

Modern security protocols and applications now predominantly rely on stronger hash functions, such as SHA-256.

Elliptic Curve Cryptography (ECC) is another encryption approach gaining prominence in recent years.

ECC is a public-key encryption technique that leverages the mathematics of elliptic curves to provide strong security with shorter key lengths compared to traditional asymmetric algorithms like RSA.

This efficiency makes ECC well-suited for resource-constrained devices and applications, such as mobile devices and IoT devices.

ECC's security is based on the elliptic curve discrete logarithm problem, which is considered computationally difficult to solve.

The adoption of ECC is increasing in various domains, including secure communications and digital signatures.

Post-Quantum Cryptography (PQC) is a field of cryptography that addresses the potential threat posed by quantum computers to existing encryption algorithms.

Quantum computers have the potential to efficiently solve certain mathematical problems that underpin the security of many encryption algorithms in use today, including RSA and ECC.

To prepare for the post-quantum era, cryptographers are developing new encryption algorithms that are resistant to quantum attacks.

These algorithms are designed to provide secure encryption even in the presence of quantum computers.

Examples of post-quantum encryption approaches include lattice-based cryptography, code-based cryptography, and multivariate polynomial cryptography.

The adoption of post-quantum cryptography will be essential as quantum computing technology continues to advance.

Homomorphic encryption is an advanced encryption technique that allows computations to be performed on encrypted data without decrypting it.

This is particularly valuable for privacy-preserving computations, where sensitive data can remain encrypted while still being processed.

Homomorphic encryption has applications in fields like healthcare, finance, and secure cloud computing.

While it offers significant advantages for data privacy, it is computationally intensive and has limitations in terms of performance.

In summary, advanced encryption algorithms play a critical role in ensuring the security and confidentiality of data in various applications.

Encryption techniques like AES, RSA, ECC, hash functions, post-quantum cryptography, and homomorphic encryption provide layers of protection against unauthorized access and cyber threats.

As the digital landscape evolves, staying informed about the latest developments in encryption technology is essential to maintaining robust security practices in an increasingly interconnected world.

Key rotation and management are crucial aspects of modern cryptographic systems, ensuring the continued security of sensitive data and communications.

In the world of encryption and security, keys are the linchpin that holds everything together, serving as the secret sauce that transforms plaintext into ciphertext and back again.

Imagine keys as the digital locks that keep your data safe, and key rotation as changing those locks periodically to reduce the risk of unauthorized access.

But why is key rotation necessary, and how can organizations effectively manage their keys to maintain security?

Let's dive into these topics and explore key rotation and management strategies.

To begin, it's essential to understand why key rotation is important.

Over time, cryptographic keys can become vulnerable to attacks, especially as computing power and attack techniques evolve.

What was considered a strong key years ago may no longer provide adequate protection against modern threats.

Key rotation addresses this vulnerability by regularly replacing old keys with new, fresh ones.

This practice ensures that even if an attacker somehow obtains an old key, it will no longer be useful because the data it encrypts is now protected by a different key.

Moreover, key rotation can mitigate the impact of data breaches.

If a breach occurs, and the attacker gains access to data and keys, regularly rotated keys limit the exposure of sensitive information.

Now that we understand why key rotation is vital let's explore some key rotation strategies.

First, there's manual key rotation, where an organization manually generates new keys and replaces old ones on a predetermined schedule.

While this approach provides control, it can be labor-intensive and error-prone, particularly for organizations with numerous keys to manage.

Another method is automated key rotation, which leverages cryptographic tools and systems to handle key updates automatically.

Automated key rotation is efficient and reduces the risk of human errors.

It's well-suited for large-scale environments where numerous keys are in use.

Some cryptographic libraries and services provide built-in key rotation mechanisms, simplifying the implementation process.

Regardless of whether an organization opts for manual or automated key rotation, it's essential to establish a clear key rotation policy.

This policy should outline the frequency of key rotation, the criteria for selecting new keys, and the processes for securely distributing and storing them.

Key rotation should be a coordinated effort involving multiple stakeholders, including IT administrators, security teams, and application developers.

Additionally, organizations should maintain a record of key rotation activities to ensure compliance with security policies and regulatory requirements.

Now, let's delve into key management, which is closely intertwined with key rotation.

Key management encompasses the practices and procedures for generating, distributing, storing, and retiring cryptographic keys.

It's the foundation upon which key rotation rests, as secure key management is essential to the success of any key rotation strategy.

To achieve robust key management, organizations should follow several best practices.

First and foremost, keys should be generated using strong, well-vetted cryptographic algorithms.

Weak or predictable keys can undermine the entire security infrastructure.

Additionally, keys must be stored securely.

This involves protecting them from unauthorized access, theft, and loss.

Hardware security modules (HSMs) are often used to provide a secure environment for key storage.

They are specialized devices designed to safeguard cryptographic keys and perform cryptographic operations securely.

Key storage solutions should also include mechanisms for auditing and logging key access and usage.

This helps organizations monitor and detect any suspicious activities related to their keys.

Moreover, access to keys should be strictly controlled.

Only authorized personnel should have access to keys, and strong access controls should be in place.

Key administrators should follow the principle of least privilege, ensuring that users have only the access they need to perform their tasks.

Furthermore, organizations should have contingency plans in place for key recovery.

In case of unexpected key loss or corruption, having a plan for key recovery can prevent data loss and downtime.

Key management systems should include robust backup and recovery procedures to ensure the availability of keys when needed.

And, of course, key rotation should be part of the key management strategy, as we discussed earlier.

In addition to these best practices, organizations should consider compliance requirements and industry standards when developing their key management policies.

Regulatory frameworks like GDPR, HIPAA, and PCI DSS may dictate specific key management and key rotation practices that organizations must adhere to.

Finally, continuous monitoring and auditing of key management processes are crucial.

Regularly reviewing and assessing key management practices can help identify vulnerabilities and improve overall security.

In summary, key rotation and management are essential components of a robust cryptographic security strategy.

Key rotation ensures that cryptographic keys remain resilient against evolving threats, and organizations can choose between manual and automated key rotation methods.

Effective key management, on the other hand, is the foundation of key rotation, encompassing practices such as key generation, storage, access control, and recovery.

By following best practices and staying compliant with regulations, organizations can establish a secure and reliable key rotation and management framework that safeguards their data and communications in an ever-changing security landscape.

Chapter 5: Advanced Network Security in Cloud Environments

Microsegmentation is a cutting-edge security strategy that's gaining prominence in today's rapidly evolving cybersecurity landscape.

It's a concept that represents a significant shift from traditional network security practices and is geared towards providing enhanced security for modern networks.

To understand microsegmentation better, let's explore what it is and why it's becoming increasingly crucial in today's digital world.

At its core, microsegmentation is a security approach that involves dividing a network into smaller, isolated segments or zones.

These segments are created based on various factors, including network traffic patterns, user roles, and security requirements.

By creating these smaller segments, organizations can control and monitor traffic flow with a level of granularity that was previously challenging to achieve.

The primary goal of microsegmentation is to improve network security by minimizing the attack surface and limiting lateral movement for potential attackers.

In traditional network security models, once an attacker breaches the perimeter or gains access to a single system, they often have the ability to move laterally across the network.

This lateral movement can lead to data breaches and significant security incidents.

Microsegmentation addresses this vulnerability by isolating network segments, making it more challenging for an attacker to move between segments even after gaining initial access.

This concept of "zero trust" networking, where trust is never assumed even within the network, is a fundamental principle of microsegmentation.

One of the key advantages of microsegmentation is the ability to enforce fine-grained access controls.

Instead of relying solely on traditional perimeter-based firewalls, organizations can implement access policies at the segment or even individual workload level.

For example, a finance department's servers can be placed in a dedicated segment with strict access controls, limiting access to only authorized personnel.

This approach reduces the attack surface and mitigates the risk of lateral movement within the network.

Microsegmentation also enhances visibility and monitoring capabilities.

With detailed segmentation, organizations can gain better insights into network traffic and detect anomalous behavior more effectively.

This visibility is critical for identifying and responding to security incidents promptly.

Moreover, microsegmentation supports compliance efforts by helping organizations enforce access policies that align with regulatory requirements.

For instance, healthcare organizations can segment their networks to separate electronic health record systems from other parts of the network, ensuring that only authorized personnel can access sensitive patient data.

Microsegmentation can be implemented using various technologies and solutions.

One common approach is to leverage software-defined networking (SDN) solutions that provide the flexibility to create and manage network segments dynamically.

SDN allows organizations to define network policies and segmentation rules in software, making it easier to adapt to changing security needs.

Additionally, some security vendors offer dedicated microsegmentation solutions that provide granular control over network traffic and access.

These solutions often include features such as intrusion detection and prevention systems (IDPS), application-aware firewalls, and traffic analysis tools.

When implementing microsegmentation, organizations should follow a well-defined process.

Start by conducting a thorough network assessment to identify existing traffic patterns, critical assets, and potential security risks.

This assessment forms the foundation for creating a segmentation strategy.

Next, determine the segmentation criteria, such as user roles, application dependencies, and data sensitivity.

Based on this criteria, define access policies for each segment, specifying who can access what resources and under what conditions.

It's essential to involve stakeholders from various departments, including IT, security, and compliance, to ensure that the segmentation strategy aligns with business needs and regulatory requirements.

Once the segmentation plan is in place, organizations can start implementing the necessary network changes.

This may involve configuring switches, routers, and firewall rules to enforce the access policies defined earlier.

Testing is a critical phase to ensure that the segmentation is working as intended and that it doesn't disrupt business operations.

Organizations should also continuously monitor and update their microsegmentation strategy as network requirements evolve.

Microsegmentation isn't a one-time project but an ongoing security practice that should adapt to changing threats and business needs.

In summary, microsegmentation is a powerful security strategy that enhances network security by creating isolated segments with fine-grained access controls.

This approach reduces the attack surface, limits lateral movement for potential attackers, and enhances visibility and monitoring capabilities.

Microsegmentation can be implemented using various technologies and solutions, and it's crucial to follow a well-defined process that includes network assessment, segmentation criteria, access policy definition, implementation, testing, and ongoing monitoring and updates.

By adopting microsegmentation, organizations can strengthen their security posture and better protect their digital assets in today's complex and dynamic threat landscape.

Cloud-native firewall solutions have emerged as essential tools for securing modern cloud environments, providing organizations with the means to protect their cloud-based assets effectively.

As more businesses transition their applications and data to the cloud, the need for robust and adaptable security measures has never been more critical.

Traditional firewalls, designed for on-premises networks, struggle to adapt to the dynamic and distributed nature of cloud computing.

Cloud-native firewalls address these challenges by offering a flexible and scalable approach to security.

But what exactly are cloud-native firewalls, and how do they differ from their traditional counterparts?

Cloud-native firewalls are a breed of firewall solutions specifically engineered to secure cloud-based infrastructure and applications.

Unlike traditional firewalls that rely on physical appliances or software installed on local servers, cloud-native firewalls are designed to be cloud-agnostic, operating seamlessly within cloud environments.

This cloud-native approach enables organizations to protect their cloud assets without the constraints of physical hardware or the need for complex configuration.

One of the primary distinctions of cloud-native firewalls is their adaptability to the dynamic nature of the cloud.

In traditional networks, firewalls are typically static, with predefined rules and configurations that may not easily accommodate changes in network topology or traffic patterns.

Cloud-native firewalls, on the other hand, are built to scale with the cloud, allowing them to adapt to shifting workloads and network changes automatically.

This adaptability ensures that security policies remain effective as cloud environments evolve.

Another key feature of cloud-native firewalls is their ability to provide visibility and control across multi-cloud and hybrid cloud environments.

With organizations increasingly adopting multi-cloud strategies or maintaining a mix of on-premises and cloud resources, it's essential to have a unified security solution that can monitor and protect assets wherever they reside.

Cloud-native firewalls offer centralized management and visibility, simplifying security administration across diverse cloud platforms.

One of the core functionalities of cloud-native firewalls is traffic inspection and filtering.

These firewalls inspect incoming and outgoing network traffic, applying security policies and rules to determine whether the traffic is permitted or should be blocked.

This inspection occurs at multiple layers of the network stack, allowing for granular control over the traffic flow.

Firewalls can filter traffic based on factors such as source and destination IP addresses, port numbers, protocols, and even the content of the data packets.

Additionally, cloud-native firewalls often integrate with threat intelligence feeds and security databases to identify and block known malicious IP addresses, domains, and patterns.

Beyond basic traffic filtering, cloud-native firewalls frequently include advanced security features such as intrusion detection and prevention systems (IDPS), application-layer filtering, and content inspection.

These capabilities enable organizations to protect against a wide range of cyber threats, including malware, zero-day exploits, and application vulnerabilities.

Moreover, cloud-native firewalls offer secure remote access and connectivity options.

As remote work becomes increasingly common, organizations need secure methods for employees, partners, and vendors to access cloud resources.

Cloud-native firewalls provide features like virtual private network (VPN) support, secure sockets layer (SSL) decryption, and multi-factor authentication (MFA) to ensure that remote access remains secure and compliant with security policies.

One significant advantage of cloud-native firewalls is their scalability.

Cloud environments are inherently scalable, and cloud-native firewalls are designed to scale seamlessly alongside cloud resources.

Whether an organization's cloud footprint grows or shrinks, cloud-native firewalls can adapt to handle the changing traffic loads and security demands.

This scalability is particularly valuable during peak traffic times or when facing sudden increases in workload.

When considering cloud-native firewalls, organizations should evaluate their ability to integrate with cloud-native security services and automation tools.

Many cloud providers offer native security services, such as AWS Web Application Firewall (WAF) or Azure Firewall, that complement cloud-native firewall solutions.

Integrating these services and automating security policies can further enhance the overall security posture.

In addition to integration, organizations should consider the management and reporting capabilities of cloud-native firewalls.

Effective security requires visibility into the network, threats, and policy enforcement.

Choose a cloud-native firewall solution that provides comprehensive reporting, alerting, and monitoring features to facilitate proactive threat detection and response.

Furthermore, compliance is a significant concern for many organizations.

Cloud-native firewalls should support compliance requirements specific to the industry or region in which the organization operates.

This may include standards such as GDPR, HIPAA, or PCI DSS.

Organizations should select cloud-native firewall solutions that offer compliance features and facilitate auditing and reporting to demonstrate adherence to regulatory requirements.

In summary, cloud-native firewall solutions are essential tools for securing modern cloud environments.

They provide adaptability, scalability, visibility, and control needed to protect cloud-based assets effectively.

By choosing the right cloud-native firewall solution and integrating it with cloud-native security services and automation tools, organizations can bolster their cloud security posture and confidently embrace the benefits of cloud computing while mitigating risks.

Chapter 6: Security Automation and Orchestration

Implementing security orchestration workflows is a crucial step in enhancing an organization's cybersecurity posture in today's complex threat landscape.

Security orchestration involves the automation of various security tasks, processes, and workflows to respond effectively to security incidents and vulnerabilities.

By streamlining and coordinating these activities, security orchestration helps organizations detect, investigate, and respond to threats rapidly and efficiently.

But what does the process of implementing security orchestration workflows entail, and why is it essential for modern cybersecurity?

Let's explore these questions to gain a better understanding of this critical topic.

First and foremost, it's vital to recognize that cybersecurity threats are continuously evolving, becoming more sophisticated and widespread.

Organizations face a constant barrage of cyberattacks, ranging from malware infections and phishing attempts to advanced persistent threats.

To defend against these threats effectively, security teams need a robust and agile approach.

This is where security orchestration comes into play.

At its core, security orchestration involves the integration of various security tools, technologies, and processes into a unified framework.

This framework enables security teams to automate routine tasks, such as incident triage, threat investigation, and response actions.

By automating these processes, organizations can significantly reduce response times, minimize human errors, and enhance overall security.

Security orchestration also enhances collaboration among security teams, allowing them to work cohesively to address security incidents.

Now, let's delve into the steps involved in implementing security orchestration workflows.

The first step is to assess the organization's current security environment.

This includes identifying existing security tools, processes, and workflows.

It's essential to understand how different security components interact and where automation can add value.

During this assessment, organizations should also define their security goals and objectives.

What specific security outcomes do they want to achieve through orchestration?

For example, organizations may aim to reduce mean time to detect (MTTD) and mean time to respond (MTTR) to security incidents.

Once the assessment is complete, organizations can start selecting the appropriate security orchestration platform or solution.

There are various security orchestration, automation, and response (SOAR) platforms available, each with its features and capabilities.

Organizations should choose a platform that aligns with their specific requirements and integrates seamlessly with their existing security stack.

Integration is a key aspect of security orchestration.

Organizations should integrate their chosen SOAR platform with their security tools, such as antivirus, intrusion detection systems, security information and event management (SIEM) systems, and endpoint protection solutions.

This integration enables the orchestration platform to communicate and coordinate actions with these tools effectively.

During the integration phase, organizations should also define the workflows and processes they want to automate.

For example, they can create workflows for handling phishing incidents, malware infections, or insider threats.

These workflows should specify the actions to be taken at each step, from initial detection to resolution.

It's essential to involve various stakeholders, including IT, security, and compliance teams, in defining these workflows to ensure they align with business needs and regulatory requirements.

Once the workflows are defined, organizations can begin building them within the SOAR platform.

This typically involves using a graphical interface to design the workflow logic, specify triggers, and define decision points.

The workflows should encompass both automated actions and manual tasks that require human intervention.

Automation is a central component of security orchestration, as it allows organizations to respond to threats in real-time.

For example, if a security alert indicates a potential malware infection, the orchestration platform can automatically isolate the affected system, initiate a malware scan, and notify the security team.

However, not all security tasks can or should be fully automated.

Human analysts still play a critical role in threat investigation and decision-making.

Therefore, orchestration workflows should include mechanisms for escalating tasks to human analysts when necessary.

These tasks may involve in-depth threat analysis, decision-making based on context, and communication with other stakeholders.

Another important consideration in implementing security orchestration workflows is monitoring and reporting.

Organizations should establish metrics and key performance indicators (KPIs) to measure the effectiveness of their orchestration efforts.

These metrics may include MTTD, MTTR, the number of incidents handled, and the accuracy of automated responses.

Regular monitoring and reporting help organizations identify areas for improvement and fine-tune their workflows for better results.

It's also crucial to conduct training and awareness programs for the security team and other stakeholders.

Orchestration workflows may change existing processes, and it's essential to ensure that everyone understands their roles and responsibilities within the new framework.

Additionally, organizations should stay informed about emerging threats and vulnerabilities to keep their orchestration workflows up to date and effective.

In summary, implementing security orchestration workflows is essential for organizations seeking to enhance their cybersecurity defenses in the face of evolving threats.

Security orchestration streamlines and automates security processes, enabling rapid threat detection, investigation, and response.

By following a structured approach that includes assessment, platform selection, integration, workflow design, monitoring, and training, organizations can effectively harness the power of security orchestration to protect their digital assets and data.

Automated incident response in cloud environments is a critical component of modern cybersecurity strategies, designed to help organizations detect, analyze, and mitigate security incidents more efficiently.

As cloud adoption continues to grow, the need for automated incident response becomes increasingly apparent, given the unique challenges posed by cloud computing.

Next, we will explore the significance of automated incident response in the cloud and how it can strengthen an organization's security posture.

To begin, it's essential to understand what automated incident response entails.

Automated incident response involves the use of technology and predefined processes to detect, analyze, and respond to security incidents without human intervention.

This approach leverages various tools and technologies, including security orchestration, automation, and response (SOAR) platforms, to execute predefined incident response workflows.

The goal is to reduce the time it takes to identify and address security threats, minimizing the potential impact of those threats on an organization's digital assets.

In cloud environments, where the scale and complexity of resources are often vast, manual incident response can be slow and inefficient.

Automated incident response addresses this challenge by providing a rapid and standardized approach to handling security incidents.

One of the key benefits of automated incident response is its ability to detect security incidents in real-time or near-real-time.

Automated monitoring tools can continuously analyze cloud traffic, logs, and events to identify abnormal or suspicious activities.

When an anomaly or security breach is detected, the automated system can trigger predefined incident response actions, such as isolating affected resources, collecting forensic data, and notifying the security team.

This real-time detection and response capability are crucial in cloud environments, where threats can evolve rapidly.

Additionally, automated incident response ensures consistency and accuracy in incident handling.

Human analysts may make errors or overlook critical steps during the incident response process, potentially leading to security gaps or delays in mitigation.

Automated workflows follow predefined procedures meticulously, reducing the risk of human error and ensuring that incident response actions are executed consistently.

Another advantage of automated incident response in the cloud is scalability.

Cloud environments can scale up or down based on demand, and security incident volumes may vary significantly.

Automated systems can adapt to handle a high volume of incidents without a corresponding increase in human resources.

This scalability is particularly valuable for organizations with dynamic and evolving cloud infrastructures.

Furthermore, automated incident response helps organizations meet compliance requirements more effectively.

Many industries and regions have specific regulations and standards governing incident response and reporting.

Automated systems can generate audit trails, incident reports, and compliance documentation with accuracy and efficiency, simplifying the compliance process.

Now, let's explore the components and steps involved in implementing automated incident response in the cloud.

The foundation of automated incident response is a well-defined incident response plan.

This plan outlines the organization's incident response policies, procedures, and responsibilities.

It should include predefined incident categories, severity levels, and response actions.

Creating this plan requires collaboration among IT, security, and compliance teams to ensure alignment with business goals and regulatory requirements.

Once the incident response plan is in place, organizations can select and implement the necessary technology stack.

This stack typically includes a SOAR platform or other automation tools, as well as integration with cloud security services and threat intelligence sources.

Integration with cloud service providers (e.g., AWS, Azure, GCP) is crucial for automated incident response in the cloud, as it allows for seamless communication and action across the entire cloud environment.

After integrating the necessary tools and services, organizations can define and implement incident response workflows.

These workflows outline the steps to be taken when specific types of security incidents occur.

For example, a workflow for a compromised virtual machine might involve isolating the VM, capturing forensic data, and notifying the security team.

It's important to customize workflows to align with the organization's unique cloud environment and security requirements.

Automation plays a central role in incident response workflows.

Organizations can automate tasks such as resource isolation, data collection, threat analysis, and communication.

Automation scripts and playbooks can be developed to execute these tasks swiftly and accurately. During this phase, organizations should also define criteria for triggering automated incident response.

These criteria are based on the analysis of security alerts, anomalies, and events generated by monitoring tools.

For instance, a sudden spike in network traffic or multiple failed login attempts may trigger an incident response workflow.

Monitoring tools should be configured to provide real-time or near-real-time alerts, enabling rapid response.

Training and awareness are essential elements of successful automated incident response.

Security and IT teams must be familiar with incident response workflows and automation tools.

Regular training exercises and simulations can help teams practice incident response procedures and improve their readiness.

Moreover, organizations should conduct continuous monitoring and tuning of automated incident response processes.

Incident response workflows may need adjustments based on the evolving threat landscape and changes in the cloud environment.

Regular reviews and updates ensure that automated incident response remains effective and aligned with security goals.

In summary, automated incident response in cloud environments is a critical capability for organizations seeking to enhance their security posture.

It provides real-time detection, rapid response, scalability, consistency, and compliance support.

By following a structured approach that includes incident response planning, technology integration, workflow definition, and ongoing monitoring and training, organizations can harness the power of automation to protect their cloud assets and respond effectively to security incidents in the ever-evolving threat landscape.

Chapter 7: Incident Response and Forensics in the Cloud

Cloud incident response frameworks are structured methodologies that help organizations effectively manage and respond to security incidents in cloud environments.

These frameworks provide a systematic approach to detecting, analyzing, mitigating, and recovering from security incidents, ensuring that organizations can minimize the impact of incidents on their cloud-based assets.

In this chapter, we will explore the significance of cloud incident response frameworks and how they play a crucial role in enhancing an organization's cloud security posture.

First and foremost, it's essential to recognize that cloud environments introduce unique challenges when it comes to incident response.

The dynamic and distributed nature of the cloud, along with the use of various cloud service models (IaaS, PaaS, SaaS), requires a tailored approach to incident response.

Cloud incident response frameworks address these challenges by providing organizations with a structured and adaptable framework for handling incidents in the cloud.

One of the key benefits of using a cloud incident response framework is that it helps organizations establish clear incident response policies and procedures.

These policies define the roles and responsibilities of various stakeholders, including IT, security, legal, and compliance teams, ensuring that everyone knows their roles during an incident.

Additionally, incident response frameworks provide guidance on classifying incidents based on severity, impact, and scope, helping organizations prioritize their response efforts.

For example, a framework may define incident categories such as data breaches, DDoS attacks, unauthorized access, or malware infections.

Each category may have predefined response procedures tailored to the specific nature of the incident.

Moreover, cloud incident response frameworks emphasize the importance of proactive incident preparation.

This includes creating incident response playbooks, developing communication plans, and conducting tabletop exercises and simulations to ensure that teams are well-prepared to respond effectively to incidents when they occur.

The use of cloud-specific incident response frameworks is essential because traditional incident response approaches may not adequately address the nuances of cloud environments.

For example, in a traditional on-premises environment, incident response may involve physical access to servers or network appliances, which is not applicable in the cloud.

Cloud incident response frameworks take into account the unique characteristics of cloud services, such as virtualization, elasticity, and shared responsibility models.

One of the widely recognized cloud incident response frameworks is the "NIST Computer Security Incident Handling Guide," which provides comprehensive guidance on incident response in cloud environments.

The National Institute of Standards and Technology (NIST) outlines a structured approach to incident response, encompassing preparation, detection, analysis, containment, eradication, recovery, and post-incident activities.

Another notable framework is the "AWS Well-Architected Framework," which includes incident response as one of its pillars.

AWS provides best practices and guidelines for building and operating secure cloud architectures, and its Well-Architected Framework includes recommendations for incident response preparedness.

Microsoft Azure offers its own set of cloud incident response resources and guidance through the Azure Security Center.

These resources cover topics such as security alerts, incident investigation, and mitigation strategies specific to Azure cloud services.

Google Cloud also provides incident response guidance, emphasizing the importance of continuous monitoring, incident detection, and response planning within its cloud environment.

In addition to these cloud provider-specific frameworks, there are industry-specific frameworks and standards that organizations can leverage.

For example, the Payment Card Industry Data Security Standard (PCI DSS) outlines requirements for incident response in the context of credit card data protection.

Similarly, the Health Insurance Portability and Accountability Act (HIPAA) includes provisions related to incident response in healthcare organizations' cloud environments.

Regardless of the specific framework used, it's important for organizations to tailor their incident response processes to their unique cloud environment, risk profile, and compliance requirements.

To effectively implement a cloud incident response framework, organizations should begin by conducting a risk assessment to identify potential threats and vulnerabilities in their cloud environment.

This assessment should consider factors such as the type of cloud services used, data sensitivity, and access controls.

Once risks are identified, organizations can develop an incident response plan that outlines the steps to be taken when incidents occur.

This plan should define incident categories, severity levels, and response procedures, as well as specify communication channels and incident reporting requirements.

Furthermore, organizations should establish an incident response team with clearly defined roles and responsibilities.

This team should include incident responders, investigators, legal counsel, and communication coordinators.

Regular training and awareness programs are essential to ensure that team members are well-prepared to respond to incidents effectively.

Incorporating automation into incident response processes can significantly improve response times and accuracy.

Automation can be used to detect and respond to common security incidents, such as malware infections or unauthorized access attempts.

Cloud incident response frameworks often recommend the use of security orchestration, automation, and response (SOAR) platforms to streamline incident response workflows and execute predefined actions.

Monitoring and continuous improvement are critical aspects of incident response.

Organizations should continuously monitor their cloud environment for security events and incidents.

This includes analyzing logs, alerts, and security telemetry data to detect abnormal activities.

Regularly reviewing and updating incident response playbooks and procedures is essential to ensure that they remain effective and aligned with the evolving threat landscape.

Conducting post-incident reviews and lessons learned sessions can help organizations identify areas for improvement and enhance their incident response capabilities.

In summary, cloud incident response frameworks play a pivotal role in helping organizations effectively manage and respond to security incidents in cloud environments.

These frameworks provide structured guidance for incident preparation, detection, analysis, containment, eradication, recovery, and post-incident activities.

By adopting and customizing cloud incident response frameworks to their specific cloud environment and compliance requirements, organizations can strengthen their cloud security posture and effectively address the unique challenges posed by cloud computing.

Digital forensics techniques for cloud environments have become increasingly important as organizations continue to migrate their data and operations to cloud platforms.

Next, we will explore the significance of digital forensics in cloud environments and the specialized techniques required to investigate and analyze incidents in these dynamic and distributed settings.

Cloud computing offers numerous benefits, including scalability, cost-efficiency, and accessibility, but it also introduces unique challenges when it comes to digital forensics.

Traditional digital forensics methods, which are designed for on-premises environments, may not be directly applicable to cloud-based investigations.

One of the key challenges in cloud digital forensics is the shared responsibility model.

In most cloud environments, cloud service providers (CSPs) are responsible for the security of the cloud infrastructure, while customers are responsible for securing their data and applications within the cloud.

This division of responsibilities means that investigators may not have direct access to certain cloud infrastructure components, making evidence collection and analysis more complex.

Furthermore, cloud environments are highly dynamic, with resources being provisioned and deprovisioned as needed.

This dynamic nature can complicate the preservation and collection of digital evidence.

Given these challenges, it's essential to adopt specialized digital forensics techniques tailored to cloud environments.

One of the foundational steps in cloud digital forensics is incident identification and notification.

When a potential security incident occurs in the cloud, organizations must promptly identify the incident, document relevant information, and notify their incident response team.

This initial step sets the stage for the subsequent forensic investigation.

Once an incident is identified, digital evidence preservation becomes a critical task.

Preservation ensures that potential evidence is protected from alteration or deletion during the investigation.

Cloud providers typically offer features for creating snapshots, backups, and logs that can serve as valuable sources of evidence.

However, investigators must act swiftly to preserve evidence, as cloud environments are subject to constant changes.

After preserving evidence, investigators can proceed with digital forensics techniques designed for cloud environments.

One such technique is remote data collection.

In cloud investigations, it may not be feasible or practical to physically access the target systems.

Remote data collection allows investigators to gather evidence from cloud resources without physical access.

This technique involves leveraging cloud provider APIs, command-line interfaces (CLIs), and scripts to collect data and logs from virtual machines, databases, and other cloud resources.

These collected artifacts can include log files, configuration settings, system snapshots, and network traffic data.

Cloud providers often offer forensic-ready services that generate logs and provide access to event data, aiding in the investigation.

Another critical aspect of cloud digital forensics is the analysis of cloud artifacts.

Cloud artifacts are digital remnants left behind by user activities and system events within the cloud environment.

These artifacts can provide valuable insights into an incident and help reconstruct the timeline of events.

Common cloud artifacts include access logs, authentication logs, audit logs, network traffic logs, and system event logs.

Analyzing these artifacts requires specialized knowledge of cloud services, APIs, and log formats.

Investigators must also be aware of the data retention policies of cloud providers, as evidence may have a limited lifespan before being automatically purged.

In addition to analyzing cloud-specific artifacts, investigators must consider cross-cloud and cross-platform investigations.

Many organizations use multiple cloud providers or hybrid cloud architectures, which can complicate forensic analysis.

In such cases, investigators need to adapt their techniques to collect and analyze evidence from diverse cloud environments.

Moreover, cloud investigations often involve collaboration between multiple parties, including cloud providers, legal teams, and law enforcement agencies.

Investigators must be prepared to navigate legal and jurisdictional complexities, ensuring that evidence is admissible in court.

Chain of custody, documentation, and adherence to legal procedures are paramount in cloud digital forensics.

Cloud-specific incident reconstruction techniques are essential for understanding the sequence of events leading up to and following a security incident.

These techniques involve mapping the actions of users and systems in the cloud to reconstruct the incident's timeline.

This process can help investigators identify the root cause of the incident, trace the attacker's actions, and assess the impact on cloud resources.

Moreover, forensic analysis of cloud storage is a crucial aspect of cloud digital forensics.

Cloud storage services, such as object storage and file storage, often contain valuable evidence related to data breaches and unauthorized access.

Investigators need to understand how to access and analyze data stored in these cloud services, including retrieving deleted files and assessing access logs.

Additionally, cloud-specific malware analysis techniques are necessary to identify and analyze malicious code or files that may have infiltrated cloud environments.

Malware analysis in the cloud requires specialized tools and expertise to examine suspicious files, identify their behavior, and determine their impact on cloud resources.

Furthermore, cloud memory forensics techniques enable investigators to analyze the memory state of cloud virtual machines.

Memory forensics can uncover valuable evidence related to running processes, open network connections, and malware presence within cloud instances.

It's worth noting that some cloud providers offer memory capture and analysis capabilities as part of their security services.

Finally, cloud incident reporting and documentation are essential for maintaining a clear record of the investigation process and findings.

Investigators should document their procedures, findings, and evidence in a systematic and organized manner.

This documentation not only supports the investigation but also serves as a crucial resource for legal proceedings and compliance requirements.

In summary, digital forensics techniques for cloud environments are indispensable in today's digital landscape.

As organizations increasingly rely on cloud services, the ability to investigate and respond to security incidents in the cloud is paramount.

Specialized techniques, such as remote data collection, artifact analysis, incident reconstruction, and memory forensics, are essential for effective cloud digital forensics.

Moreover, investigators must navigate the challenges posed by the shared responsibility model, dynamic nature of cloud environments, and legal considerations to ensure a successful investigation.

By embracing these specialized techniques and staying abreast of cloud security developments, organizations can enhance their ability to detect, investigate, and mitigate security incidents in the cloud.

Chapter 8: Advanced Compliance and Governance

Cloud compliance automation is a crucial aspect of modern cloud security and governance practices.

It refers to the use of automated tools and processes to ensure that an organization's cloud resources and operations comply with relevant regulatory standards, industry best practices, and internal policies.

In today's highly regulated and dynamic cloud environments, manual compliance checks and audits are often insufficient to maintain the required levels of security and adherence to compliance standards.

Cloud compliance automation helps organizations address this challenge by providing a systematic and efficient way to continuously monitor, assess, and enforce compliance across their cloud infrastructure.

At its core, cloud compliance automation is about reducing the burden of compliance management on IT and security teams while improving accuracy and agility.

Traditional compliance efforts often involve manual tasks, such as collecting and reviewing logs, conducting security assessments, and generating compliance reports.

These tasks can be time-consuming, error-prone, and resource-intensive.

In contrast, cloud compliance automation leverages cloud-native tools and third-party solutions to streamline and automate compliance-related activities.

One of the primary benefits of cloud compliance automation is its ability to provide real-time visibility into the compliance status of cloud resources.

Automated compliance tools continuously monitor cloud environments, checking configurations, access controls, and security settings against predefined compliance policies.

When a deviation from compliance is detected, these tools can trigger alerts and corrective actions in near real-time.

This proactive approach allows organizations to address compliance issues promptly, reducing the risk of security incidents and non-compliance penalties.

Cloud compliance automation also supports the concept of "infrastructure as code" (IaC), where cloud resources are defined and managed through code.

IaC allows organizations to define compliance policies as code, ensuring that compliance requirements are embedded directly into the provisioning and configuration of cloud resources.

When cloud resources are created or modified, the compliance policies defined in code are automatically applied, minimizing the risk of misconfigurations and compliance gaps.

Another essential aspect of cloud compliance automation is its ability to provide audit trails and documentation.

Compliance audits are a common requirement for organizations subject to regulatory standards like PCI DSS, HIPAA, GDPR, and others.

Cloud compliance automation tools generate detailed audit logs and reports that demonstrate compliance efforts, helping organizations prove their adherence to regulations during audits.

Moreover, automation can accelerate the audit process itself by providing auditors with easy access to compliance data and evidence.

Cloud compliance automation tools often offer predefined compliance templates and frameworks that organizations can leverage.

These templates are designed to align with specific regulations and industry standards, making it easier for organizations to adopt and implement compliance best practices.

Organizations can customize these templates to match their specific requirements and policies while still benefiting from the foundational compliance framework provided.

One of the key challenges that cloud compliance automation addresses is the complexity of multi-cloud and hybrid cloud environments.

Many organizations use a combination of cloud providers and on-premises infrastructure, making compliance management more challenging due to diverse technologies and configurations.

Cloud compliance automation tools are designed to work seamlessly across multiple cloud platforms and on-premises environments, providing a centralized and standardized approach to compliance management.

Additionally, they support the concept of "single pane of glass" visibility, where organizations can view and manage compliance for all their resources from a unified dashboard.

The ability to automate compliance checks and remediation actions is a significant advantage of cloud compliance automation.

When non-compliance issues are detected, automation tools can execute predefined remediation actions to bring resources back into compliance.

For example, if a cloud instance is found to have insecure firewall rules, the automation tool can automatically adjust the rules to align with the organization's security policies.

This proactive approach ensures that security and compliance are continuously enforced without manual intervention.

Furthermore, cloud compliance automation promotes a culture of "compliance as code."

This means that compliance policies, checks, and remediation actions are codified and version-controlled, similar to application code.

As a result, compliance becomes an integral part of an organization's DevOps and DevSecOps processes.

This approach enables security and compliance to be integrated into the software development and deployment pipelines, reducing the risk of compliance issues emerging during application development and release.

Organizations can also leverage cloud compliance automation for risk assessment and mitigation.

By continuously monitoring compliance status and identifying areas of non-compliance, organizations can proactively assess their security and compliance risks.

Automation tools can prioritize remediation actions based on risk levels, helping organizations focus their efforts on the most critical areas.

Additionally, cloud compliance automation can provide documentation and evidence of risk assessment and mitigation efforts, which can be valuable for risk management and reporting.

In summary, cloud compliance automation is a critical component of modern cloud security and governance.

It empowers organizations to proactively monitor, assess, and enforce compliance across their cloud environments, reducing manual effort, improving accuracy, and ensuring continuous compliance.

By automating compliance checks, remediation actions, and documentation, organizations can enhance their security posture, reduce compliance risks, and streamline compliance management in multi-cloud and hybrid cloud environments.

Chapter 9: DevSecOps and Cloud Security

Integrating security into DevOps pipelines is a critical step in modern software development practices, as it helps organizations build and deploy secure applications more efficiently.

In today's fast-paced digital landscape, the traditional approach of treating security as a separate phase in the development process is no longer sufficient.

Instead, security must be integrated throughout the entire DevOps pipeline, from code development to deployment and beyond.

This shift-left approach to security ensures that potential vulnerabilities are identified and addressed early in the development process, reducing the risk of security breaches and costly post-release fixes.

One of the fundamental principles of integrating security into DevOps pipelines is to automate security testing.

Automated security testing tools and techniques, such as static application security testing (SAST), dynamic application security testing (DAST), and interactive application security testing (IAST), can scan code and applications for security flaws and vulnerabilities.

These tools can be seamlessly integrated into the CI/CD (Continuous Integration/Continuous Deployment) pipeline, allowing security checks to occur automatically whenever code changes are made.

By automating security testing, developers can receive immediate feedback on security issues, enabling them to fix vulnerabilities before they propagate further downstream.

Another critical aspect of integrating security into DevOps pipelines is the use of container security scanning.

Containers have become a popular choice for packaging and deploying applications due to their lightweight nature and portability.

However, containers also introduce unique security challenges.

Container security scanning tools can analyze container images for known vulnerabilities and misconfigurations.

These scans can be integrated into the CI/CD process, ensuring that only secure container images are deployed into production environments.

Furthermore, security orchestration and automation play a crucial role in DevOps security.

Security orchestration involves the coordination and management of various security tools and processes to respond to security incidents and automate security-related tasks.

Automation, on the other hand, focuses on scripting and automating repetitive security tasks, such as patching systems, applying security configurations, and responding to alerts.

Together, security orchestration and automation help organizations respond to security incidents more effectively and reduce manual intervention.

DevSecOps is a cultural and organizational shift that promotes collaboration between development, security, and operations teams.

It emphasizes the shared responsibility for security and the need for security professionals to work closely with developers and operations staff.

By embedding security experts within DevOps teams, organizations can proactively address security concerns throughout the development lifecycle.

Security experts can provide guidance on secure coding practices, conduct security reviews, and assist with threat modeling.

DevSecOps also encourages the use of security as code, where security policies and controls are defined and enforced through code.

Infrastructure as code (IaC) tools, such as Terraform and Ansible, allow organizations to codify their infrastructure and security configurations.

By implementing security as code, organizations can ensure that security controls are consistently applied across all environments, from development to production.

Continuous monitoring is another vital aspect of integrating security into DevOps pipelines.

Security teams should continuously monitor applications and infrastructure for anomalies and potential security threats.

This includes monitoring logs, network traffic, and system behavior.

DevOps pipelines can be configured to trigger alerts and automated responses based on predefined security policies and detection criteria.

Continuous monitoring not only helps detect security incidents but also provides valuable data for threat analysis and incident response.

One of the challenges organizations face when integrating security into DevOps pipelines is the need to balance security and agility.

DevOps is all about delivering software quickly, and security checks can sometimes introduce delays.

To address this challenge, organizations can implement risk-based security testing.

Risk-based security testing involves prioritizing security tests based on the potential impact and likelihood of exploitation.

High-risk areas of the application may undergo more extensive testing, while lower-risk areas may receive less scrutiny.

By focusing security efforts where they are most needed, organizations can strike a balance between security and agility.

Additionally, organizations should embrace the concept of security champions within development teams.

Security champions are developers who have a strong interest in security and receive specialized training in security best practices.

These champions act as a bridge between development and security teams, helping to disseminate security knowledge and practices throughout the organization.

By nurturing security champions, organizations can create a culture of security awareness and responsibility.

Finally, it's essential to have clear security policies and procedures in place as part of the integration of security into DevOps pipelines.

These policies should define security standards, acceptable practices, and incident response procedures.

All team members should be aware of these policies and follow them as part of their daily work.

Regular security training and awareness programs can also help reinforce these policies and keep teams informed about the latest security threats and best practices.

In summary, integrating security into DevOps pipelines is essential for building and deploying secure software in today's fast-paced digital environment.

By automating security testing, implementing container security scanning, embracing security as code, and fostering a DevSecOps culture, organizations can proactively address security concerns throughout the development lifecycle.

Continuous monitoring, risk-based testing, and security champions further enhance the security posture while balancing agility.

Clear security policies and training programs ensure that security is a shared responsibility among all team members, ultimately leading to more resilient and secure applications.

Security as code is a fundamental concept in the DevSecOps approach to software development and deployment.

It represents the integration of security practices and controls directly into the software development process, treating security as an integral part of the application's codebase.

Traditionally, security has often been seen as an afterthought in software development, with security assessments and controls applied after the application has been built.

However, this approach can lead to vulnerabilities being discovered late in the development cycle, resulting in costly and time-consuming remediation efforts.

Security as code aims to shift security left in the development process, meaning that security considerations are addressed from the very beginning, during the design and coding phases.

One of the key benefits of implementing security as code is the early identification and mitigation of security vulnerabilities.

By incorporating security checks into the development pipeline, developers receive immediate feedback on potential security issues as they write code.

Static code analysis tools, for example, can scan the codebase for common security flaws and provide real-time feedback to developers.

This enables developers to fix security issues before they become entrenched in the application, reducing the overall risk of security breaches.

Furthermore, security as code helps enforce consistent security policies and practices across the entire development team.

Security controls and best practices are codified as rules and guidelines that developers must follow during the development process.

These rules can cover various aspects of security, such as input validation, authentication, authorization, and data encryption.

By codifying security policies, organizations ensure that security is not subject to interpretation or oversight, leading to more robust and consistent security practices.

Security as code also promotes the use of automation in security processes.

Automated security testing tools and scripts can be integrated into the continuous integration/continuous deployment (CI/CD) pipeline, enabling the automated scanning of code for vulnerabilities.

This automation accelerates the security assessment process, making it feasible to conduct security checks with every code change, no matter how frequent.

Moreover, automation can assist in the enforcement of security policies, automatically applying security controls and configurations to cloud resources and infrastructure.

Another advantage of security as code is the ability to version and track security configurations alongside the application code.

Infrastructure as code (IaC) tools allow organizations to define and manage infrastructure and security configurations using code.

This means that security configurations become part of the application's codebase, subject to version control and change tracking.

As a result, organizations can maintain an audit trail of security changes and ensure that security configurations are consistent across development, testing, and production environments.

Additionally, security as code facilitates collaboration between development and security teams.

Security experts can work closely with developers to define security requirements and guidelines, helping developers understand and implement security best practices.

This collaborative approach fosters a culture of shared responsibility for security and encourages cross-functional teams to work together to achieve secure software.

Security as code also aligns well with the principles of DevSecOps, a cultural and organizational shift that emphasizes security in every phase of the DevOps lifecycle.

In a DevSecOps environment, security professionals are integrated into development and operations teams, providing expertise and guidance on security matters.

By treating security as code, organizations can seamlessly integrate security practices into the DevOps pipeline, enabling continuous security assessments and remediation.

However, implementing security as code may come with challenges.

One challenge is the need for security expertise within the development team.

Developers must understand security principles and be able to implement security controls effectively.

Training and education programs can bridge this knowledge gap and empower developers to take ownership of security as code.

Another challenge is the potential for false positives in automated security testing.

Automated tools may generate alerts for potential security issues that are not actual vulnerabilities.

Therefore, it's crucial to fine-tune and customize security checks to reduce false positives and ensure that developers focus on genuine security risks.

Finally, organizations need to invest in the development and maintenance of security policies and controls as code.

This includes defining security rules, creating security testing scripts, and continuously updating security policies to adapt to evolving threats and regulations.

In summary, security as code is a foundational concept in DevSecOps that emphasizes integrating security practices and controls directly into the software development process.

By identifying and mitigating security vulnerabilities early, enforcing consistent security policies, and leveraging automation, organizations can build more secure applications.

Security as code also encourages collaboration between development and security teams, fostering a culture of shared responsibility for security.

While challenges exist, the benefits of security as code far outweigh the drawbacks, ultimately leading to more resilient and secure software in today's rapidly evolving threat landscape.

Chapter 10: Emerging Trends and Future Challenges in Cloud Security

Cloud-native security technologies are at the forefront of defending modern cloud-based applications and infrastructure.

These technologies are specifically designed to protect cloud-native environments, which differ significantly from traditional on-premises data centers.

One key characteristic of cloud-native applications is their reliance on microservices architecture.

In a microservices architecture, applications are composed of small, independently deployable services that communicate through APIs.

This architecture allows for greater flexibility and scalability but also introduces new security challenges.

To address these challenges, container security has become a crucial component of cloud-native security.

Containers, such as Docker, are a popular choice for packaging and deploying microservices.

Container security technologies provide mechanisms to secure containerized applications by scanning container images for vulnerabilities, controlling access to containers, and monitoring container runtime behavior.

Container orchestration platforms like Kubernetes have also gained prominence in cloud-native environments.

These platforms help manage and scale containers, but they require robust security measures.

Kubernetes security technologies focus on securing the Kubernetes control plane, managing access control, and protecting the network and storage configurations of Kubernetes clusters.

Another fundamental aspect of cloud-native security is identity and access management.

In cloud-native environments, numerous entities, including services, applications, and users, interact with cloud resources.

Identity and access management technologies help ensure that only authorized entities can access resources and that their permissions are limited to what is necessary.

Cloud providers offer identity and access management services, such as AWS Identity and Access Management (IAM) and Azure Active Directory (AD), that allow fine-grained control over resource access.

Encryption is a critical component of cloud-native security.

Data encryption technologies, including encryption in transit and encryption at rest, help protect sensitive data from unauthorized access.

Cloud providers typically offer encryption services and tools for managing encryption keys securely.

Cloud-native security also encompasses cloud workload protection.

This involves securing virtual machines, containers, and serverless functions running in the cloud.

Security solutions for cloud workloads monitor for suspicious activity, detect vulnerabilities, and provide real-time threat detection and response.

Cloud-native security technologies often leverage machine learning and artificial intelligence to detect and mitigate threats more effectively.

Security information and event management (SIEM) solutions tailored for cloud environments are becoming increasingly prevalent.

These SIEM solutions collect and analyze logs and security events from cloud services, applications, and infrastructure to detect and respond to security incidents.

Continuous security monitoring is a fundamental practice in cloud-native security.

Tools and technologies continuously monitor cloud environments for signs of security breaches, unauthorized access, and unusual behavior.

Automated responses can be triggered when anomalies are detected, helping mitigate security risks quickly.

Cloud-native security also extends to serverless computing.

Serverless computing platforms, like AWS Lambda and Azure Functions, have unique security considerations.

Security technologies for serverless environments focus on monitoring function execution, controlling access to resources, and ensuring that function code is free from vulnerabilities.

Security as code is an emerging concept in cloud-native security.

It involves defining security policies and configurations as code and integrating them into the CI/CD pipeline.

As code changes are deployed, security policies are automatically enforced, reducing the risk of misconfigurations and security breaches.

In summary, cloud-native security technologies are a vital part of securing modern cloud-based applications and infrastructure.

They address the unique challenges posed by microservices architecture, containerization, and serverless computing.

These technologies encompass container security, Kubernetes security, identity and access management, encryption, cloud workload protection, machine learning-based threat detection, SIEM for the cloud, continuous monitoring, and security as code.

By embracing cloud-native security technologies, organizations can protect their cloud resources effectively and stay ahead of evolving security threats in the dynamic cloud environment.

Artificial Intelligence (AI) and Machine Learning (ML) have revolutionized cloud security, offering advanced capabilities to protect against evolving threats.

These technologies are making a significant impact by enhancing threat detection, automating incident response, and improving overall security posture.

In the realm of threat detection, AI and ML are invaluable.

They can analyze massive volumes of data, such as network traffic logs and application behavior, to identify patterns and anomalies that may indicate security breaches.

This capability enables organizations to detect and respond to threats more quickly than traditional methods.

AI and ML can also improve the accuracy of threat detection by reducing false positives, helping security teams focus on genuine security risks.

Intrusion detection and prevention systems (IDPS) powered by AI can identify new and previously unknown attack patterns, offering a proactive defense against emerging threats.

Moreover, AI and ML can play a crucial role in user and entity behavior analytics (UEBA).

By analyzing user and entity behavior, these technologies can identify unusual or suspicious activities that may indicate compromised accounts or insider threats.

UEBA solutions can provide insights into risky behavior patterns, enabling organizations to take timely action to mitigate risks.

AI and ML also enhance security through automation.

Automated incident response is becoming more common, where AI-driven systems can detect and respond to security incidents without human intervention.

For example, AI-powered chatbots can analyze and respond to user inquiries regarding security policies, password resets, or account access, reducing the workload on security teams.

In addition, AI-driven security orchestration and automation platforms can automatically trigger predefined responses to specific security events, such as isolating compromised devices or blocking malicious IP addresses.

By automating incident response, organizations can reduce response times and improve overall security resilience.

Machine learning is instrumental in improving endpoint security.

Endpoint detection and response (EDR) solutions leverage ML algorithms to detect and respond to threats on individual devices.

These algorithms can identify unusual behavior on endpoints, such as suspicious processes or file changes, and take automated actions to contain and mitigate threats.

Furthermore, AI and ML can enhance cloud security by improving the accuracy of identity and access management.

Behavior-based access control, driven by ML, can analyze user behavior patterns to determine if access requests are legitimate or potentially malicious.

This approach can help prevent unauthorized access and reduce the risk of credential theft.

AI and ML are also being utilized to enhance email security.

Machine learning models can analyze email content and attachments to identify phishing attempts, malware, and other email-borne threats.

By automatically detecting and blocking malicious emails, these technologies reduce the risk of successful email-based attacks.

In cloud security, AI and ML can provide insights into cloud resource misconfigurations and vulnerabilities.

Cloud security posture management (CSPM) solutions use ML algorithms to scan cloud environments for misconfigurations, compliance violations, and security gaps.

These solutions can provide automated recommendations for remediation, helping organizations maintain a strong security posture.

AI-driven threat intelligence is another valuable application.

Machine learning models can analyze vast amounts of threat data to identify emerging threats and vulnerabilities.

By providing actionable threat intelligence, organizations can proactively address security risks before they are exploited by attackers.

In the realm of security information and event management (SIEM), AI and ML are transforming the way security events are analyzed.

ML algorithms can process and correlate large volumes of security data, helping SIEM solutions detect and respond to complex attack patterns.

They can identify deviations from normal behavior and generate alerts for further investigation.

AI-driven SIEM solutions can also automate incident response actions based on predefined playbooks, streamlining security operations.

AI and ML are not without challenges in cloud security.

One challenge is the need for high-quality, labeled training data to train machine learning models effectively.

Without sufficient data, ML algorithms may struggle to accurately detect threats and anomalies.

Additionally, organizations must consider the ethical implications of AI and ML in security.

Bias in ML models can lead to discriminatory outcomes, and transparency in AI decision-making is essential.

Therefore, organizations should carefully evaluate and monitor AI and ML solutions to ensure fairness and accountability.

In summary, AI and ML are transformative technologies in cloud security.

They enhance threat detection, automate incident response, improve identity and access management, enhance email security, bolster endpoint security, and provide valuable insights into cloud security posture.

However, organizations must address challenges related to data quality and ethics to harness the full potential of AI and ML in cloud security.

By embracing these technologies, organizations can stay ahead of evolving threats and protect their cloud environments effectively.

BOOK 3
CLOUD SECURITY AND FORENSICS
INVESTIGATING INCIDENTS IN AZURE, AWS, AND GCP

ROB BOTWRIGHT

Chapter 1: Introduction to Cloud Security Incidents

Cloud security incidents come in various forms, each posing unique challenges to organizations in maintaining the integrity, availability, and confidentiality of their cloud resources.

One common type of cloud security incident is unauthorized access, where malicious actors gain unauthorized entry to cloud systems or data.

This can happen through compromised credentials, weak passwords, or vulnerabilities in authentication mechanisms.

Unauthorized access incidents can lead to data breaches, data theft, and unauthorized modifications.

Another prevalent cloud security incident is data breaches, where sensitive data is exposed to unauthorized parties.

Data breaches can result from various factors, including misconfigured cloud storage, unpatched vulnerabilities, or insider threats.

When data breaches occur, organizations may face legal and reputational consequences.

Denial-of-service (DoS) and distributed denial-of-service (DDoS) attacks are also significant cloud security incidents.

These attacks aim to overwhelm cloud services or applications, rendering them unavailable to users.

DoS and DDoS attacks can disrupt operations and cause financial losses.

Phishing attacks are a persistent threat in cloud security.

In phishing incidents, attackers trick users into revealing sensitive information, such as login credentials or personal data.

Phishing emails or websites can mimic trusted sources, making them difficult to detect.

Phishing incidents can lead to unauthorized access or data theft.

Malware and ransomware attacks are critical cloud security incidents that involve the deployment of malicious software on cloud resources.

Malware can steal data, spy on users, or disrupt cloud services.

Ransomware incidents encrypt data and demand a ransom for decryption keys.

Both types of attacks can lead to data loss and financial extortion.

Cloud misconfigurations are a prevalent type of cloud security incident caused by human error or oversight.

Misconfigurations can expose sensitive data, cloud storage, or resources to unauthorized access.

Attackers often scan for misconfigured cloud instances to exploit them.

Insider threats involve malicious actions or negligence by individuals within an organization.

Insiders may intentionally or unintentionally compromise cloud security by sharing sensitive data or misconfiguring resources.

These incidents are challenging to detect and prevent.

Cryptojacking is an emerging cloud security incident where attackers use cloud resources to mine cryptocurrencies without authorization.

It can lead to resource depletion, increased costs, and performance degradation.

Web application attacks, such as SQL injection and cross-site scripting (XSS), target vulnerabilities in cloud-hosted web applications.

These incidents can compromise sensitive data and expose users to risks.

Account compromise incidents involve the unauthorized access of user accounts.

Attackers may steal login credentials or use social engineering techniques to gain access.

Once compromised, accounts can be misused for various purposes.

Data loss or leakage incidents involve the accidental or intentional exposure of sensitive data.

This can happen through misconfigured sharing settings, email errors, or data transfer mistakes.

Data loss incidents can lead to compliance violations and reputational damage.

These are just some of the many types of cloud security incidents organizations may encounter.

To effectively mitigate these risks, organizations should implement comprehensive cloud security measures, including access controls, monitoring, encryption, and employee training.

Furthermore, organizations must stay vigilant, continuously assess their cloud security posture, and adapt their defenses to the evolving threat landscape.

Understanding the various types of cloud security incidents is a crucial step in building a robust and proactive security strategy.

The impact of cloud security incidents can be profound, affecting organizations in multiple ways, from financial losses to reputational damage.

One significant impact is financial, as cloud security incidents can result in direct financial losses for organizations.

For instance, data breaches may lead to regulatory fines, legal fees, and the cost of notifying affected individuals.

Additionally, organizations may incur expenses to investigate and remediate security incidents.

The financial impact can extend to lost revenue if the incident disrupts operations, leading to downtime or a loss of customers' trust.

Reputational damage is another severe consequence of cloud security incidents.

When organizations suffer data breaches or other security incidents, their reputation can be tarnished, eroding the trust of customers, partners, and stakeholders.

Rebuilding a damaged reputation can be challenging and time-consuming.

Lost business opportunities can result from cloud security incidents.

Customers who lose trust in an organization's ability to protect their data may take their business elsewhere.

This loss of customers can have long-term financial consequences.

Legal and regulatory consequences are significant impacts of cloud security incidents.

Organizations may face lawsuits from affected parties, regulatory investigations, and compliance violations.

These legal and regulatory issues can lead to substantial penalties and damage an organization's standing.

Cloud security incidents can also result in data loss or theft, which can have severe consequences.

Lost or stolen data can include sensitive customer information, intellectual property, or proprietary data.

The loss of such data can lead to a competitive disadvantage or intellectual property theft.

Operational disruptions are another notable impact.

Distributed denial-of-service (DDoS) attacks, for example, can render cloud services unavailable, affecting business operations and customer satisfaction.

Organizations may incur additional costs to restore normal operations and bolster security.

In some cases, cloud security incidents can lead to the exposure of sensitive intellectual property or trade secrets.

Competitors or malicious actors may use this information to gain a competitive advantage or engage in industrial espionage.

The exposure of valuable intellectual property can harm an organization's future prospects.

Cloud security incidents can also impact an organization's ability to meet contractual obligations.

When security incidents disrupt services or data availability, organizations may fail to deliver on service-level agreements (SLAs) with customers or partners.

This breach of contractual obligations can result in legal disputes and financial penalties.

Employee morale and productivity can be affected by cloud security incidents.

When employees are aware of security breaches or incidents, it can create a sense of unease and distraction, leading to decreased productivity.

Moreover, employees may lose trust in their organization's ability to protect their personal information.

In some cases, cloud security incidents may lead to the departure of valuable talent.

Insurance premiums may increase for organizations that have experienced cloud security incidents.

Insurers view organizations with a history of security incidents as higher-risk clients and may adjust premiums accordingly.

These increased costs can further strain an organization's financial resources.

Another significant impact of cloud security incidents is the time and effort required for remediation.

Incident response efforts, forensic investigations, and security enhancements can be time-consuming and resource-intensive.

During this process, organizations may divert resources from other critical business activities.

Organizations that fail to respond effectively to cloud security incidents may experience a prolonged impact, with ongoing security vulnerabilities or the recurrence of incidents.

In summary, the impact of cloud security incidents can be far-reaching and multifaceted.

It includes financial losses, reputational damage, lost business opportunities, legal and regulatory consequences, data loss or theft, operational disruptions, intellectual property exposure, contractual breaches, employee morale and productivity issues, increased insurance premiums, and the resource-intensive nature of remediation efforts.

Understanding these impacts underscores the importance of robust cloud security measures and proactive incident response strategies for organizations operating in the cloud.

Chapter 2: Incident Detection and Response

Real-time incident monitoring is a crucial aspect of an effective cloud security strategy, enabling organizations to detect and respond to security threats as they happen.

This proactive approach allows organizations to minimize the impact of security incidents and reduce potential damage.

Real-time incident monitoring involves continuously monitoring cloud environments for unusual or suspicious activities, such as unauthorized access attempts, data breaches, or malware infections.

By analyzing incoming data and events in real-time, security teams can quickly identify security incidents and take immediate action to mitigate them.

One of the primary benefits of real-time incident monitoring is its ability to provide early detection of security threats.

Instead of waiting for periodic security assessments or audits, organizations can receive immediate alerts when suspicious activities occur.

This early warning system allows security teams to respond swiftly and prevent security incidents from escalating.

Moreover, real-time incident monitoring enhances the visibility of cloud environments.

It provides a comprehensive view of all activities and events happening within the cloud, making it easier to detect anomalies or patterns indicative of security threats.

This increased visibility is essential in today's complex and dynamic cloud landscapes.

To achieve real-time incident monitoring, organizations typically deploy security information and event management (SIEM) systems, intrusion detection systems (IDS), and security orchestration platforms.

These tools collect and analyze vast amounts of data from various sources, such as logs, network traffic, and cloud resources.

Machine learning and artificial intelligence (AI) algorithms can assist in identifying potential security threats and anomalies.

Once a security incident is detected in real-time, the incident response process kicks into action.

Security teams can assess the severity of the incident, gather additional context, and initiate the appropriate response actions.

Response actions may include isolating compromised systems, blocking malicious IP addresses, or escalating the incident for further investigation.

Furthermore, real-time incident monitoring is essential for compliance and regulatory requirements.

Many industry regulations and standards mandate continuous monitoring and real-time incident response capabilities.

Meeting these requirements not only ensures compliance but also enhances an organization's overall security posture.

Cloud service providers (CSPs) also offer real-time monitoring and alerting capabilities as part of their cloud security services.

These native tools provide organizations with visibility into the security of their cloud resources and applications.

However, organizations should complement these native tools with third-party solutions to achieve comprehensive and centralized incident monitoring.

It's important to note that real-time incident monitoring is not limited to on-premises resources.

Organizations must extend their monitoring capabilities to encompass multi-cloud and hybrid cloud environments.

These complex cloud architectures require a unified approach to incident monitoring, allowing organizations to detect and respond to threats regardless of where they occur.

In multi-cloud environments, data and workloads may span multiple cloud providers, making centralized monitoring even more critical.

To effectively implement real-time incident monitoring, organizations must establish clear incident response processes and workflows.

This includes defining roles and responsibilities within the incident response team, documenting response procedures, and conducting regular training and drills.

Automation can also play a significant role in real-time incident monitoring.

Automated incident response workflows can accelerate response times and reduce the risk of human error.

Furthermore, organizations should continuously review and refine their incident monitoring capabilities.

As threats evolve, so should incident detection and response strategies.

Regularly updating detection rules, fine-tuning AI algorithms, and adapting to emerging threats are all essential components of effective real-time incident monitoring.

In summary, real-time incident monitoring is a critical component of modern cloud security strategies.

It enables organizations to detect and respond to security threats as they happen, providing early warning and rapid response capabilities.

To implement effective real-time incident monitoring, organizations should leverage advanced tools, establish clear incident response processes, and adapt to the evolving threat landscape.

By doing so, organizations can enhance their cloud security posture and protect their valuable assets in the cloud.

Incident response strategies and protocols are fundamental to effectively handling security incidents in a structured and coordinated manner.

These strategies provide a clear roadmap for identifying, assessing, mitigating, and recovering from security incidents.

In today's digital landscape, where cyber threats are constant and evolving, having a well-defined incident response plan is crucial for minimizing the impact of incidents.

Incident response strategies begin with preparation, where organizations proactively establish a dedicated incident response team and define their roles and responsibilities.

This team is responsible for managing and executing the incident response process when an incident occurs.

In addition to forming the response team, organizations should develop an incident response policy that outlines the overarching goals and objectives of the incident response program.

This policy sets the tone for how incidents will be handled within the organization and aligns with broader security and compliance objectives.

Furthermore, organizations should establish an incident response plan, which is a detailed document that provides step-by-step instructions for responding to specific types of incidents.

This plan includes procedures for incident detection, notification, containment, eradication, recovery, and lessons learned.

Having a well-documented plan ensures that response efforts are consistent and efficient.

As part of their incident response strategies, organizations must also consider legal and regulatory requirements.

Many industries and jurisdictions have specific regulations that dictate how incidents must be reported and handled.

Therefore, incident response strategies should align with these legal and regulatory requirements to avoid potential penalties and legal issues.

Moreover, organizations must ensure that their incident response strategies are flexible and scalable.

Cyber threats are constantly evolving, and incident response plans should be able to adapt to new attack vectors and techniques.

Regular testing and drills are essential components of effective incident response strategies.

Organizations should conduct tabletop exercises and simulated incident scenarios to evaluate the effectiveness of their plans, identify weaknesses, and train the response team.

Once an incident occurs, the incident response strategies and protocols kick into action.

The first phase of incident response is detection, where security tools and monitoring systems are used to identify potential incidents.

This phase also involves recognizing unusual patterns or activities that may indicate a security threat.

Once an incident is detected, it must be reported promptly to the incident response team.

Notification is a critical step in incident response, and organizations should have clear procedures for reporting incidents to the response team and, if required, external authorities or regulators.

After notification, the incident response team must assess the severity and scope of the incident.

This assessment helps determine the appropriate level of response and allocation of resources.

Containment is the next phase, where the response team takes actions to prevent the incident from spreading or causing further damage.

This may involve isolating compromised systems, changing passwords, or blocking malicious IP addresses.

Eradication follows containment and involves identifying the root cause of the incident and permanently removing it from the environment.

Recovery is the final phase of incident response, where the organization works to restore affected systems and services to normal operation.

This phase may also include data restoration and ensuring that vulnerabilities that led to the incident are addressed to prevent future occurrences.

Throughout the incident response process, documentation is crucial.

The response team should maintain detailed records of all actions taken, communications, and findings.

These records not only provide a historical record of the incident but also support post-incident analysis and reporting.

In addition to the immediate response phases, incident response strategies should include a post-incident phase.

This phase involves analyzing the incident to identify lessons learned and areas for improvement.

Organizations should conduct a thorough post-mortem analysis to understand how the incident occurred, what could have been done differently, and how to enhance incident response capabilities.

Incident response strategies should be regularly reviewed and updated to reflect changes in the threat landscape, technology, and regulatory requirements.

Continuous improvement is essential for maintaining effective incident response capabilities.

In summary, incident response strategies and protocols are essential components of a comprehensive cybersecurity program.

They provide a structured approach to detecting, assessing, mitigating, and recovering from security incidents.

By developing and implementing well-defined incident response strategies, organizations can minimize the impact of incidents and enhance their overall cybersecurity posture.

Chapter 3: Cloud Forensics Fundamentals

Understanding the principles of cloud forensics is vital in today's digital landscape, where cloud computing plays a central role in businesses and organizations.

Cloud forensics is the practice of collecting, preserving, analyzing, and presenting digital evidence from cloud environments to investigate and respond to security incidents and legal matters.

These principles provide a foundation for conducting effective cloud forensics investigations.

One fundamental principle of cloud forensics is the recognition that cloud environments are unique and distinct from traditional on-premises infrastructure.

Cloud services are dynamic and elastic, allowing organizations to scale resources up and down rapidly.

This dynamic nature presents challenges for investigators, as cloud environments are in a constant state of change.

As a result, cloud forensics requires specialized knowledge and techniques to address these challenges effectively.

Another principle of cloud forensics is the importance of understanding the shared responsibility model between cloud service providers (CSPs) and cloud customers.

In most cloud environments, CSPs are responsible for the security of the cloud infrastructure, while customers are responsible for securing their data and applications within the cloud.

This division of responsibility impacts the scope of cloud forensics investigations and the types of evidence that may be accessible.

Investigators must be aware of the limitations imposed by the shared responsibility model and work within those constraints.

Furthermore, cloud forensics investigations must be conducted with a focus on preserving the integrity and admissibility of digital evidence.

Maintaining a chain of custody and ensuring that evidence remains unchanged throughout the investigation process is essential.

This principle aligns with established forensic practices, but it takes on added importance in the context of cloud environments, where evidence can be distributed across multiple locations and jurisdictions.

Cloud forensics also places a premium on the ability to collect and analyze digital evidence remotely.

Traditional forensic practices often involve physically accessing the hardware or systems under investigation, but this may not be possible in cloud environments.

Investigators must develop remote collection techniques and leverage cloud-native tools and APIs to acquire evidence without compromising the integrity of the cloud environment.

Another key principle is the importance of documenting the cloud environment thoroughly.

This includes creating detailed records of cloud configurations, settings, and access controls, as well as tracking changes made to the environment over time.

Documentation serves as a critical reference point during cloud forensics investigations, helping investigators understand the context in which an incident occurred.

Furthermore, investigators must have a solid understanding of cloud-specific logging and monitoring capabilities.

Cloud service providers generate extensive logs and telemetry data, which can provide valuable evidence during an investigation.

Being able to identify and access these logs, as well as interpret the data they contain, is crucial in cloud forensics.

Moreover, investigators must be prepared to work with CSPs and legal authorities to obtain evidence and navigate jurisdictional challenges.

Cloud environments often span multiple regions and countries, and data may be subject to various privacy and data protection regulations.

Understanding the legal and regulatory landscape is essential for ensuring that evidence collected is admissible in court and complies with applicable laws.

In addition, cloud forensics investigations should be conducted in a manner that minimizes disruption to ongoing operations.

Cloud environments are business-critical, and any investigation should aim to limit the impact on the organization's ability to deliver services.

Balancing the need for investigation with the need for business continuity is a key principle in cloud forensics.

Lastly, cloud forensics requires ongoing training and education.

Cloud technology is continually evolving, and investigators must stay current with the latest developments in cloud services, security, and forensic techniques.

Continued learning and professional development are essential to maintaining the skills and knowledge needed to conduct effective cloud forensics investigations.

In summary, the principles of cloud forensics provide a framework for conducting investigations in cloud environments effectively.

Understanding the unique challenges and nuances of cloud computing, as well as the shared responsibility model and legal considerations, is essential for investigators working in this dynamic and rapidly evolving field.

By adhering to these principles and staying current with industry developments, investigators can successfully navigate the complexities of cloud forensics and contribute to the security and integrity of cloud-based systems and data.

Digital evidence handling in the cloud is a critical aspect of forensic investigations conducted in cloud environments.

The handling of digital evidence, whether in traditional or cloud contexts, must adhere to rigorous standards and best practices to maintain its integrity and admissibility.

In cloud environments, digital evidence can take various forms, including logs, virtual machine snapshots, configuration settings, and user activity records.

Handling this evidence effectively requires specialized knowledge and tools tailored to cloud forensics.

One fundamental aspect of digital evidence handling in the cloud is the need for a well-defined and documented process.

This process outlines the steps involved in collecting, preserving, analyzing, and presenting digital evidence.

Having a clear process in place ensures that investigators follow consistent procedures, which is crucial for maintaining the chain of custody and demonstrating the credibility of the evidence in legal proceedings.

In cloud environments, where data and systems are distributed across multiple locations and service providers, the process must be adaptable to the unique challenges posed by the cloud.

When collecting digital evidence in the cloud, investigators should prioritize the preservation of data integrity.

This involves ensuring that evidence remains unchanged and tamper-proof throughout the collection and analysis process.

Any alteration or corruption of evidence could render it inadmissible in court and undermine the credibility of the investigation.

To achieve this, investigators often use specialized tools and techniques to create forensic copies of digital evidence.

These copies are exact replicas of the original data, and they are used for analysis, leaving the original evidence intact.

Additionally, the handling of digital evidence in the cloud should consider the principles of live forensics.

In some cases, it may not be feasible to power down or isolate cloud instances for evidence collection, as this could disrupt critical business operations.

Live forensics techniques enable investigators to collect evidence from running cloud systems without impacting their functionality.

This requires careful planning and the use of tools and methods that can access and extract evidence while the systems are in operation.

Chain of custody is a central concept in digital evidence handling, regardless of the environment.

It involves maintaining a documented record of all individuals who have had custody of the evidence, from its initial collection to its presentation in court.

In cloud forensics, chain of custody is particularly challenging, given the distributed nature of cloud data and the involvement of multiple parties.

Investigators must meticulously document every step of evidence handling, including who accessed it, when, and for what purpose.

Furthermore, cloud environments often involve a shared responsibility model between cloud service providers (CSPs) and customers.

This model necessitates collaboration between investigators, CSPs, and cloud customers to ensure that evidence is accessible and properly handled.

Investigators must be aware of the legal and regulatory considerations that may impact the handling of digital evidence in the cloud.

Data privacy laws, data sovereignty requirements, and cross-border data transfer restrictions can all influence how evidence is collected and transferred during an investigation.

Navigating these legal complexities requires a deep understanding of both cloud technology and relevant regulations.

In some cases, investigators may need to obtain legal assistance to ensure compliance with applicable laws.

Moreover, digital evidence in the cloud may be subject to encryption or other security measures.

Decrypting or accessing encrypted data as part of an investigation may require specialized knowledge and cooperation from cloud service providers.

Ensuring that the evidence remains admissible while dealing with encryption is a delicate balance.

Throughout the process of handling digital evidence in the cloud, documentation is paramount.

Investigators should maintain detailed records of every action taken, every tool used, and every individual involved in the investigation.

These records serve as a trail of accountability and transparency, which is essential for maintaining the integrity of the evidence and demonstrating due diligence in court.

Lastly, training and expertise are vital components of effective digital evidence handling in the cloud.

Cloud forensics is a specialized field that demands in-depth knowledge of cloud technology, security, and investigative techniques.

Investigative teams should include individuals with the expertise to navigate the complexities of cloud environments and digital evidence.

Continued training and professional development ensure that investigators stay current with evolving cloud technologies and forensic methodologies.

In summary, digital evidence handling in the cloud is a multifaceted and challenging process that demands adherence to rigorous standards, specialized knowledge, and careful coordination.

Maintaining the integrity and admissibility of evidence in cloud environments requires a clear and adaptable process, meticulous documentation, and a deep understanding of both cloud technology and legal considerations.

By following best practices and staying informed about developments in cloud forensics, investigators can effectively handle digital evidence in the cloud and contribute to successful investigations and legal proceedings.

Chapter 4: Collecting and Preserving Cloud Evidence

In cloud forensics, evidence collection techniques are essential for gathering digital evidence from cloud environments.

These techniques are specifically designed to address the unique challenges posed by cloud computing.

Cloud environments are dynamic and distributed, making evidence collection a complex and specialized process.

One common technique in cloud evidence collection is the use of cloud-native APIs (Application Programming Interfaces).

Cloud service providers (CSPs) often offer APIs that allow investigators to access and retrieve data and logs directly from the cloud environment.

These APIs provide a secure and programmatic way to gather evidence without disrupting the operation of cloud services.

However, using cloud-native APIs requires expertise in both the specific CSP's APIs and cloud forensics techniques.

Another technique is the acquisition of virtual machine (VM) snapshots.

VMs are fundamental building blocks in cloud computing, and they encapsulate the entire state of a virtualized system, including memory, disk, and network configurations.

Investigators can capture snapshots of VMs at a particular point in time, preserving their state for forensic analysis.

This technique is particularly valuable for volatile evidence, such as running processes and volatile memory.

Cloud service providers may offer tools or APIs for creating VM snapshots, and investigators must follow proper procedures to ensure the integrity of the evidence.

Log analysis is a crucial evidence collection technique in cloud forensics.

Cloud environments generate extensive logs and telemetry data, which can provide valuable evidence for investigations. Investigators must identify relevant logs, collect them, and analyze the data they contain to reconstruct events and uncover evidence of suspicious activities.

Log analysis may involve using cloud-native log management tools or third-party log analysis solutions.

Furthermore, memory analysis is a technique used to examine the contents of a VM's memory, including the RAM (Random Access Memory).

Memory analysis can reveal valuable information about running processes, network connections, and data in use at the time of an incident.

Investigators can acquire memory dumps from VMs or cloud instances and analyze them using specialized tools.

However, memory analysis requires a deep understanding of memory structures and forensic techniques.

Another evidence collection technique in cloud environments is the preservation of configuration settings.

Cloud services are highly configurable, and settings play a crucial role in determining the behavior and security of cloud resources.

Investigators should document and preserve the configuration settings of relevant cloud services and resources.

Changes to configurations may have a significant impact on the investigation, as they can alter the behavior of cloud services and data storage.

Preserving configuration settings helps maintain the context of the investigation and ensures that investigators can understand how cloud resources were configured at the time of the incident.

In some cases, investigators may need to capture network traffic as part of evidence collection.

Network packet captures can provide insights into communication patterns, data transfers, and potential security breaches.

This technique involves capturing network traffic between cloud instances or between cloud instances and external endpoints.

Tools such as packet sniffers or network monitoring solutions can be used to capture and analyze network traffic.

However, network traffic captures may raise privacy and legal considerations, so investigators must ensure compliance with applicable laws and regulations.

Additionally, cloud storage forensics is a technique focused on gathering evidence from cloud storage services.

Cloud environments often rely on various storage solutions, including object storage, block storage, and file storage.

Investigators may need to access and analyze data stored in these cloud storage services to uncover evidence.

This may involve retrieving files, analyzing metadata, and reconstructing data access patterns.

Cloud storage forensics requires familiarity with the specific storage services used in the cloud environment.

Furthermore, live forensics is a technique that enables investigators to collect evidence from running cloud instances without disrupting their operation.

In cloud environments, it may not be feasible to shut down or isolate instances for evidence collection, as this could impact critical business operations.

Live forensics techniques allow investigators to access and gather evidence from live systems while they continue to function.

This often involves acquiring memory dumps, analyzing running processes, and monitoring network connections.

However, live forensics requires specialized tools and knowledge to avoid altering the state of the systems under investigation.

Lastly, the technique of metadata analysis involves examining metadata associated with cloud resources and data objects.

Metadata can provide valuable context and evidence in an investigation.

Investigators should gather and analyze metadata related to cloud instances, files, user access, and configuration changes.

Metadata analysis can help establish timelines, track user activities, and identify potential anomalies.

Overall, evidence collection techniques in cloud environments are diverse and require a combination of technical expertise, specialized tools, and a deep understanding of cloud technology.

Each technique serves a specific purpose in gathering digital evidence for cloud forensics investigations.

Investigators must carefully choose and execute the appropriate techniques based on the nature of the incident and the cloud environment under investigation.

Chain of custody in cloud forensics is a critical concept that ensures the integrity, authenticity, and admissibility of digital evidence collected during investigations.

It is a documented trail that accounts for the possession, control, transfer, and analysis of evidence from the moment it is collected until its presentation in court.

The chain of custody establishes a clear and unbroken record of who had access to the evidence and what actions were taken, maintaining its reliability throughout the investigative process.

In cloud forensics, the chain of custody is especially challenging due to the dynamic and distributed nature of cloud environments.

Digital evidence can exist in multiple locations across different cloud service providers (CSPs), complicating the tracking and management of custody.

One of the first steps in establishing a chain of custody is the proper labeling and documentation of evidence.

Each piece of digital evidence must be assigned a unique identifier and tagged with information such as the date, time, location, and the name of the investigator who collected it.

This labeling ensures that evidence can be identified and tracked throughout the investigative process.

Moreover, documentation is not limited to physical evidence containers, as it extends to digital files and logs collected from cloud environments.

Cloud-native tools and services often provide built-in features for generating digital evidence logs, which should be preserved and documented as part of the chain of custody.

To maintain the chain of custody in cloud forensics, it is crucial to establish a clear handover process when evidence is transferred between individuals or organizations.

This handover should include a signed acknowledgment and a record of the condition of the evidence at the time of transfer.

In cloud investigations, evidence may be transferred between cloud service providers, investigators, legal teams, or third-party forensic experts.

Each transfer should be documented and logged to ensure that the chain of custody remains unbroken.

Chain of custody records should also include detailed information about the storage and security measures in place to protect the evidence.

This includes specifying where and how evidence is stored, who has access to it, and the measures taken to prevent tampering or unauthorized alterations.

In cloud environments, digital evidence may be stored on virtual machines, in cloud storage services, or within CSP-managed environments.

Ensuring the security and integrity of evidence during storage is a critical aspect of maintaining the chain of custody.

Moreover, the chain of custody documentation should account for every action taken during the investigative process.

This includes the analysis, examination, and testing of digital evidence.

Every time evidence is accessed, examined, or manipulated, it must be thoroughly documented to provide a complete record of what was done and by whom.

In cloud forensics, where multiple parties may be involved, it is essential to track and document each action to maintain transparency and accountability.

Additionally, any changes made to the evidence, such as decryption or data extraction, must be recorded in the chain of custody documentation.

These changes should include the rationale for the alterations and the methodology used to preserve the evidence's integrity.

In the cloud, encryption is a common security measure, and decrypting evidence for analysis is a significant step in many investigations.

This decryption process should be well-documented to ensure that the chain of custody remains unbroken.

Furthermore, chain of custody records should reflect any challenges, issues, or discrepancies encountered during the investigative process.

If evidence is lost, damaged, or compromised in any way, these incidents should be documented, and efforts to mitigate or address the issues should be recorded.

Maintaining transparency regarding challenges and issues is essential for maintaining the credibility of the chain of custody.

Throughout the chain of custody process, it is essential to have a designated custodian or custodians responsible for the evidence's security and integrity.

These individuals are entrusted with safeguarding the evidence and ensuring that it remains in a pristine and unaltered state.

In cloud forensics, custodians may include cloud service providers, forensic experts, or internal investigators.

They play a critical role in adhering to the established chain of custody procedures and preserving the evidence's integrity.

Finally, the chain of custody documentation should be organized, well-maintained, and readily accessible.

These records serve as a historical account of the evidence's journey from collection to presentation in court.

Having organized and easily accessible documentation is essential for investigators, legal teams, and judges who rely on the chain of custody to assess the reliability of digital evidence.

In summary, the chain of custody is a foundational concept in cloud forensics that ensures the reliability and admissibility of digital evidence in court.

It involves labeling, documenting, and tracking evidence from collection through analysis while maintaining security and integrity.

In the dynamic and distributed nature of cloud environments, maintaining a robust chain of custody is crucial for successful investigations and legal proceedings.

Chapter 5: Analyzing Cloud Logs and Artifacts

Log analysis tools and techniques are fundamental to understanding the behavior, performance, and security of computer systems and applications.

Logs are records of events or activities that occur within an IT environment, and they provide valuable insights into system operations.

In this chapter, we will explore the importance of log analysis, various log types, and the tools and techniques used to extract actionable information from logs.

Logs serve as a historical record of events, errors, and activities, making them a crucial resource for diagnosing issues, monitoring system health, and investigating security incidents.

They can contain information about user actions, system configurations, network traffic, application errors, and security events.

By analyzing logs, organizations can gain a comprehensive view of their IT environment's operational status and security posture.

To effectively analyze logs, it's essential to understand the different types of logs generated by various components within an IT environment.

Common log types include system logs, application logs, security logs, network logs, and audit logs.

System logs record information about the operating system's activities, such as startup and shutdown events, hardware errors, and system resource usage.

Application logs capture details about software applications, including errors, warnings, user interactions, and performance metrics.

Security logs provide critical information related to security incidents, such as login attempts, authentication failures, and access control events.

Network logs document network traffic, including source and destination addresses, protocols used, and traffic patterns.

Audit logs track changes made to system configurations, user activities, and security-related events for compliance and forensic purposes.

Analyzing logs manually can be time-consuming and challenging, especially in large and complex IT environments.

Therefore, organizations leverage log analysis tools to streamline the process and extract meaningful insights from log data efficiently.

These tools come in various forms, from open-source solutions to commercial software, each offering unique features and capabilities.

Open-source log analysis tools, such as Elasticsearch, Logstash, and Kibana (ELK Stack), provide a cost-effective way to centralize and analyze log data.

They offer powerful search and visualization capabilities, allowing users to query logs, create custom dashboards, and detect anomalies.

Commercial log analysis solutions, like Splunk and Sumo Logic, offer advanced features and scalability for organizations with extensive log data needs.

They provide real-time monitoring, machine learning-driven analytics, and security information and event management (SIEM) capabilities.

One essential technique in log analysis is log aggregation, where logs from various sources are collected and centralized into a single repository.

This aggregation simplifies log management and enables a comprehensive view of an organization's IT environment.

Common log aggregation techniques include using log forwarders, syslog servers, and log collection agents to gather logs from different sources and send them to a central location.

Another crucial technique is log parsing, which involves breaking down log entries into structured data for easier analysis.

Parsing extracts relevant information, such as timestamps, event types, and error messages, from unstructured log data.

Regular expressions and parsing libraries are commonly used to achieve this.

Once logs are aggregated and parsed, analysts can perform log analysis to identify trends, anomalies, and potential security threats.

This involves searching, filtering, and correlating log data to uncover patterns or events of interest.

For example, security analysts may search for multiple failed login attempts from the same IP address within a short timeframe, indicating a potential brute-force attack.

To automate log analysis and detection of security incidents, organizations often employ alerting mechanisms.

Alerts can be triggered when specific log entries match predefined criteria or thresholds, allowing for real-time response to potential threats.

Visualization is another essential technique in log analysis, as it helps analysts understand log data quickly.

Dashboards and graphs provide a visual representation of log data trends, making it easier to identify unusual patterns or deviations from normal behavior.

Effective log analysis also involves the use of machine learning and artificial intelligence (AI) algorithms to detect anomalies and security threats.

These algorithms can identify patterns that may be difficult for human analysts to recognize and provide early warnings of potential issues.

Furthermore, log analysis should incorporate historical data to establish baseline behavior and identify deviations from that baseline.

This historical perspective enables the detection of long-term trends and gradual changes in the IT environment, which may be indicative of security incidents.

In addition to traditional log analysis techniques, organizations should consider log retention and compliance requirements.

Many industries and regulatory bodies have specific requirements regarding the retention and protection of log data.

Compliance with these regulations is essential to avoid legal and financial consequences.

Effective log management and analysis play a crucial role in meeting compliance requirements.

To conclude, log analysis is a vital practice for organizations looking to maintain the security and operational health of their IT environments.

By understanding the types of logs, utilizing log analysis tools and techniques, and incorporating automation and visualization, organizations can extract valuable insights from log data, detect security incidents, and respond proactively to potential threats.

Artifact examination is a critical phase in cloud investigations, as it involves the analysis of digital evidence collected from cloud environments.

Digital artifacts are traces of user activities, system events, and data interactions that can provide valuable insights into a case.

In cloud investigations, artifacts can be found in various forms, including logs, metadata, configuration settings, and user activity records.

The examination of these artifacts plays a significant role in uncovering the truth and understanding the sequence of events that transpired within a cloud environment.

During artifact examination, investigators follow a systematic process to collect, preserve, and analyze digital evidence.

The first step is to identify and document the sources of potential artifacts within the cloud environment.

This may include cloud service provider (CSP) logs, user account activity, configuration changes, network traffic records, and application logs.

Once the sources are identified, investigators use proper techniques to collect and preserve the evidence to ensure its integrity and admissibility in legal proceedings.

Cloud service providers often have their own mechanisms for providing logs and evidence, and investigators must work within the framework provided by the CSP.

After collecting the evidence, the next phase involves the actual examination of artifacts to extract relevant information.

This examination can be a complex process, as cloud environments generate vast amounts of data, and investigators must sift through it to find pertinent details.

One essential aspect of artifact examination is timeline analysis, where investigators create a chronological sequence of events based on the timestamps and logs.

Timeline analysis helps reconstruct what happened and when, which is crucial for understanding the case.

Investigators also use various tools and techniques to extract information from artifacts, such as log parsers, forensic software, and custom scripts.

These tools aid in the extraction of data related to user activities, system events, network traffic, and configuration changes.

Moreover, investigators look for indicators of compromise (IoCs) within the artifacts to identify potential security breaches or unauthorized access.

IoCs may include suspicious IP addresses, unexpected login attempts, or anomalies in user behavior.

During the examination, investigators pay close attention to access logs, authentication records, and privilege escalation events to identify any signs of unauthorized access or malicious activity.

In addition to examining logs and user activities, investigators often analyze metadata associated with cloud artifacts.

Metadata can provide valuable context, such as file creation and modification times, email headers, and document access history.

Metadata analysis can help reconstruct the user's actions and interactions with cloud resources.

Investigators also look for evidence of data exfiltration or leakage, which may be present in the form of file transfer logs, email logs, or document access logs.

Detecting unauthorized data movement is crucial for understanding the extent of a security incident.

During artifact examination, investigators must adhere to established forensic principles, including the preservation of the original evidence to maintain its integrity.

They create forensic copies of artifacts and work with these copies to prevent any alteration or contamination of the original data.

Additionally, investigators maintain a detailed chain of custody to document the handling and transfer of evidence, ensuring its admissibility in legal proceedings.

Artifact examination is often a collaborative effort that involves various experts, including forensic analysts, network administrators, and legal professionals.

These experts work together to analyze artifacts, interpret findings, and provide context to the evidence.

Moreover, investigators must consider the legal and ethical aspects of artifact examination, ensuring that their actions comply with privacy laws and regulations.

This includes obtaining proper legal authorization when necessary, such as search warrants or subpoenas.

Furthermore, investigators must be prepared to testify in court regarding their findings and the methodology used during artifact examination.

To summarize, artifact examination is a crucial phase in cloud investigations, where digital evidence is collected, preserved, and analyzed to uncover the truth behind security incidents or other cloud-related cases.

Investigators follow a systematic process to identify sources of evidence, collect and preserve it, and then analyze it to reconstruct events and identify potential security breaches or unauthorized activities.

Adherence to forensic principles, collaboration among experts, and compliance with legal and ethical considerations are essential aspects of successful artifact examination in cloud investigations.

Chapter 6: Investigating Identity and Access Breaches

User account compromises in the cloud pose significant security risks and are a critical concern for organizations relying on cloud services.

These compromises occur when unauthorized individuals gain access to legitimate user accounts, potentially leading to data breaches, financial losses, and reputational damage.

User account compromises can take various forms, including stolen credentials, weak passwords, and social engineering attacks.

One common method is credential theft, where malicious actors acquire a user's login credentials through phishing emails, malware, or other deceptive techniques.

Phishing emails often appear legitimate, enticing users to enter their usernames and passwords on fake websites, unknowingly providing attackers with access to their accounts.

Malware, on the other hand, can capture keystrokes or steal stored passwords, giving attackers a means to infiltrate cloud accounts.

Weak or easily guessable passwords are another vulnerability that can lead to user account compromises.

Many users still use passwords that are simple or easily guessable, such as "password123" or "admin."

Attackers can exploit these weak passwords through brute-force attacks or by using password-cracking tools.

Social engineering attacks involve manipulating individuals into divulging their login credentials or other sensitive information.

Attackers may impersonate trusted entities, use psychological tactics, or exploit trust to trick users into revealing their passwords or providing access to their accounts.

Once attackers gain access to a user's account, they often engage in various malicious activities, such as data theft, data manipulation, or unauthorized access to sensitive resources.

Data theft can involve stealing sensitive files, confidential documents, or personal information stored within the cloud environment.

Attackers may download, exfiltrate, or even delete valuable data, causing significant harm to the organization.

Data manipulation involves unauthorized changes to data, which can lead to data corruption, financial fraud, or compliance violations.

Attackers may alter financial records, customer data, or critical business documents, affecting the organization's integrity and operations.

Unauthorized access to sensitive resources within the cloud can give attackers control over critical infrastructure or systems.

This can lead to further attacks, such as launching distributed denial-of-service (DDoS) attacks, disrupting services, or compromising additional accounts.

Detecting user account compromises in the cloud is challenging due to the dynamic and distributed nature of cloud environments.

Traditional security mechanisms like firewalls and intrusion detection systems may not provide sufficient visibility into cloud-based threats.

To address this challenge, organizations need advanced threat detection and monitoring solutions designed for cloud environments.

These solutions analyze user behavior, monitor logins and access patterns, and apply machine learning algorithms to detect anomalies indicative of a compromise.

User account compromises can be difficult to detect because attackers often attempt to blend in with legitimate user activity.

Therefore, it is essential to establish a baseline of normal user behavior and continuously monitor for deviations from this baseline.

Organizations should implement multi-factor authentication (MFA) as a fundamental security measure to protect against user account compromises.

MFA requires users to provide multiple forms of verification before granting access, adding an extra layer of security beyond passwords.

Implementing strong password policies, enforcing regular password changes, and educating users about phishing and social engineering threats are also critical steps in mitigating user account compromises.

Regular security training and awareness programs can help employees recognize phishing attempts and respond appropriately.

Additionally, organizations should regularly review and audit user account permissions and access privileges.

Unused or unnecessary privileges should be revoked to reduce the attack surface and limit the potential impact of compromised accounts.

Organizations must have an incident response plan in place to quickly respond to and contain user account compromises when they occur.

This plan should include steps for isolating affected accounts, investigating the extent of the compromise, and notifying affected parties.

Legal and regulatory requirements may also dictate the need to report certain types of breaches to authorities or affected individuals.

In summary, user account compromises in the cloud pose significant threats to organizations, potentially leading to data breaches, financial losses, and damage to reputation.

These compromises can result from stolen credentials, weak passwords, or social engineering attacks.

To mitigate the risk of user account compromises, organizations should implement multi-factor authentication, strong password policies, and regular security training.

Advanced threat detection and monitoring solutions tailored to cloud environments are essential for detecting and responding to compromises effectively.

Insider threat investigations in cloud environments are a crucial aspect of maintaining security and preventing potential data breaches.

Insider threats involve individuals within an organization who misuse their access privileges to compromise data or systems, and these threats can be particularly challenging to detect and address.

These individuals may have legitimate access to sensitive information, making it difficult to distinguish between malicious activity and normal operations.

Insider threat investigations aim to uncover and mitigate the risks posed by employees, contractors, or partners who may intentionally or unintentionally compromise cloud security.

One common scenario in insider threat investigations is when an employee abuses their access to steal confidential data, intellectual property, or customer information.

This type of breach can have severe consequences, including financial losses and damage to the organization's reputation.

Another scenario involves employees who inadvertently expose sensitive data by mishandling it or falling victim to phishing attacks, allowing malicious actors to gain access to cloud resources.

Effective insider threat investigations require a systematic and proactive approach, starting with the establishment of robust security policies and procedures.

Organizations should clearly define acceptable use policies, access controls, and data handling guidelines to create a strong foundation for preventing insider threats.

Training and awareness programs play a crucial role in educating employees about security risks and best practices, helping them recognize potential threats and respond appropriately.

Investigations into insider threats often begin with the identification of suspicious behavior or unusual activities within the cloud environment.

This can include accessing sensitive data without a legitimate business reason, attempting to bypass security controls, or exhibiting unusual patterns of behavior.

To facilitate early detection, organizations should implement monitoring and logging mechanisms that capture relevant data and user activity within the cloud infrastructure.

These logs can serve as valuable sources of information during investigations, helping security teams identify potential insider threats and gather evidence.

Advanced security analytics and machine learning technologies can aid in the detection of anomalous behavior by analyzing large volumes of data to identify patterns indicative of insider threats.

When a potential insider threat is detected, investigators should gather evidence to assess the situation further.

This may involve reviewing access logs, examining email communications, and collecting digital artifacts that can provide insights into the individual's actions and intentions.

In some cases, investigators may need to conduct interviews or interrogations to gain a better understanding of the situation and the motivations behind the insider threat.

While conducting insider threat investigations, it is essential to adhere to legal and ethical guidelines, respecting the privacy and rights of individuals involved.

Organizations must strike a balance between protecting their assets and respecting the rights of employees, contractors, and partners.

In situations where insider threats lead to criminal activities, organizations may need to involve law enforcement agencies to pursue legal actions.

Once the investigation is complete, organizations must take appropriate actions to mitigate the threat and prevent future incidents.

This may involve revoking access privileges, implementing additional security controls, or, in severe cases, terminating the employment of the individual responsible for the insider threat.

An essential aspect of insider threat investigations is continuous improvement.

Organizations should regularly review and refine their security policies and procedures based on lessons learned from past incidents.

This iterative process allows organizations to adapt to evolving threats and minimize the risk of insider threats in the future.

Collaboration between different departments within an organization is crucial for effective insider threat investigations.

Security teams, human resources, legal departments, and senior management must work together to address insider threats comprehensively.

Sharing information and insights across departments enables a more holistic approach to identifying, mitigating, and preventing insider threats.

Additionally, organizations should consider investing in technologies that enhance insider threat detection and prevention.

These technologies can include user and entity behavior analytics (UEBA) solutions, data loss prevention (DLP) tools, and advanced security information and event management (SIEM) systems.

By leveraging these technologies, organizations can proactively identify potential insider threats and respond more effectively.

In summary, insider threat investigations in cloud environments are essential for safeguarding an organization's data, reputation, and financial stability.

Insider threats can manifest in various forms, including intentional malicious actions and unintentional mishandling of data.

To address these threats, organizations must establish robust security policies, provide comprehensive training and awareness programs, and implement advanced monitoring and analytics tools.

By taking a proactive and collaborative approach, organizations can better detect, investigate, and mitigate insider threats, reducing the risk of security breaches and data loss.

Chapter 7: Data Breach Investigations in the Cloud

Data exfiltration analysis is a critical component of incident response in cloud environments, aimed at understanding how unauthorized parties have removed sensitive information from an organization's cloud infrastructure.

Incidents involving data exfiltration can have severe consequences, including data breaches, financial losses, and damage to an organization's reputation.

The primary goal of data exfiltration analysis is to determine what data was compromised, how it was accessed, and who might be responsible for the breach.

Analyzing data exfiltration incidents requires a systematic approach, starting with the identification of the breach itself.

Common indicators of data exfiltration include unusual network traffic patterns, unauthorized access to sensitive data, or suspicious activities observed within the cloud environment.

Once a potential data exfiltration incident is identified, it is crucial to gather evidence to understand the extent of the breach and the methods employed by the malicious actor.

This evidence may include logs of network traffic, system access records, and data transfer activity.

Analyzing network traffic logs can reveal anomalies such as large data transfers to unfamiliar or unauthorized destinations, which may indicate data exfiltration.

Access records can provide insights into which accounts were used to access the compromised data and when these access events occurred.

Additionally, examining data transfer activity logs can help determine the volume and nature of the data that was exfiltrated.

In some cases, it may be necessary to conduct a forensic analysis of compromised systems to uncover digital artifacts left behind by the malicious actor.

This analysis can involve examining file metadata, examining system memory, and searching for traces of malware or malicious scripts.

The goal is to reconstruct the sequence of events leading up to the data exfiltration and identify any vulnerabilities or security weaknesses that were exploited.

One crucial aspect of data exfiltration analysis is establishing a timeline of events.

Creating a timeline can help investigators understand the sequence of actions taken by the malicious actor and how they managed to exfiltrate the data.

This timeline can be constructed using various pieces of evidence, such as access logs, network logs, and system activity records.

By aligning these pieces of evidence chronologically, investigators can gain a clearer picture of the breach.

Determining the scope of the data exfiltration is another critical aspect of the analysis.

Investigators need to identify what specific data was compromised, whether it contained sensitive information, and the potential impact on the organization.

This may involve working closely with data owners and stakeholders to understand the data's value and significance.

The analysis should also aim to identify potential points of entry or vulnerabilities that were exploited by the malicious actor.

This includes examining the security controls and configurations of the cloud environment, looking for misconfigurations, weak access controls, or unpatched vulnerabilities.

Understanding how the attacker gained access can help organizations bolster their security measures to prevent future incidents.

Attribution, while challenging, is also an important aspect of data exfiltration analysis.

Investigators may attempt to determine who the malicious actor or group responsible for the breach is.

Attribution can be challenging in the cloud environment, as attackers often employ various tactics to conceal their identities and origins.

However, clues such as the tools used, the attack methods employed, or the timing of the breach can provide insights into the threat actor's capabilities and motivations.

Coordinating with law enforcement or threat intelligence organizations may also yield valuable information for attribution.

Once the data exfiltration incident has been analyzed and understood, organizations must take immediate action to contain the breach and mitigate further damage.

This may involve isolating compromised systems, revoking unauthorized access, and implementing additional security measures.

Communication is also crucial during this phase, as organizations need to notify affected parties, including customers, partners, and regulatory authorities, about the breach.

Finally, organizations should conduct a post-incident review to identify lessons learned and opportunities for improvement.

This review should encompass not only the technical aspects of the incident but also the organization's response and communication strategies.

By learning from the incident, organizations can strengthen their security posture and better prepare for future data exfiltration incidents.

In summary, data exfiltration analysis is a vital component of incident response in cloud environments.

It involves identifying and understanding how unauthorized parties have removed sensitive information, determining the scope and impact of the breach, and taking actions to contain and mitigate the incident.

Analyzing data exfiltration incidents requires a systematic approach, including the establishment of timelines, the identification of vulnerabilities, and potential attribution of the threat actor.

By conducting thorough data exfiltration analysis and learning from each incident, organizations can enhance their overall security posture and reduce the risk of future breaches.

When a data breach occurs, it is crucial to respond promptly and effectively to mitigate the damage and prevent further unauthorized access.

Remediation efforts involve identifying and addressing the vulnerabilities or weaknesses that allowed the breach to happen in the first place.

This process starts with containing the breach by isolating compromised systems or accounts to prevent the attacker from continuing their activities.

The containment phase aims to limit the attacker's access to the organization's systems and data.

Next, organizations must conduct a thorough investigation to understand the extent of the breach and the data that was compromised.

This often involves digital forensics techniques to collect and analyze evidence, reconstruct the timeline of events, and determine how the breach occurred.

During the investigation, organizations should work closely with legal and regulatory experts to ensure compliance with data breach notification laws and regulations.

Once the investigation is complete, organizations should take steps to remediate the vulnerabilities that allowed the breach to happen.

This may involve patching or updating software, strengthening access controls, and improving security configurations.

It is essential to address the root causes of the breach to prevent similar incidents from occurring in the future.

During the remediation process, organizations should also assess the impact of the breach on affected individuals and notify them in accordance with legal requirements.

Clear and transparent communication with affected parties is crucial to maintaining trust and transparency.

In addition to technical remediation, organizations should also review their security policies and procedures to identify areas for improvement.

This may involve revising incident response plans, updating security awareness training, and conducting security assessments.

Continuous monitoring and threat intelligence should be used to detect any signs of ongoing malicious activity or future attacks.

Reporting the data breach to the appropriate authorities and regulatory bodies is often required by law.

Organizations should work closely with legal counsel to ensure that they meet all reporting obligations and comply with data protection regulations.

The timing and content of breach notifications may vary depending on jurisdiction, so organizations must be well-informed about the specific requirements in their region.

In addition to reporting to regulatory authorities, organizations should also communicate the breach to their customers, partners, and other stakeholders as necessary.

Transparency is key to maintaining trust, and affected parties should be informed promptly and provided with information on how to protect themselves from potential harm.

In some cases, organizations may offer credit monitoring or identity theft protection services to affected individuals as a goodwill gesture.

Public relations and communication experts can help craft the messages and responses required during a data breach, ensuring that the organization's reputation is managed effectively.

In the aftermath of a data breach, organizations should also evaluate their incident response efforts and conduct a post-incident review.

This review should encompass the technical, procedural, and communication aspects of the incident response.

Identifying lessons learned and areas for improvement is essential to strengthening an organization's security posture.

It is crucial to adapt and evolve security measures based on the insights gained from each data breach.

Furthermore, organizations should review their cyber insurance policies to understand coverage and ensure that they have adequate protection in place.

Cyber insurance can help mitigate financial losses resulting from a data breach, including legal expenses, regulatory fines, and costs associated with breach notifications.

In summary, remediation and reporting in data breaches are essential components of an effective incident response strategy.

Organizations must respond swiftly to contain the breach, conduct thorough investigations, and remediate vulnerabilities to prevent future incidents.

Clear and transparent communication with affected parties and regulatory authorities is crucial, as is compliance with data breach notification laws.

Continuous monitoring, threat intelligence, and post-incident reviews are essential for ongoing security improvement.

Chapter 8: Network Forensics in Cloud Environments

Understanding and analyzing network traffic in a cloud environment is vital for maintaining security and performance.

Cloud network traffic analysis involves monitoring and examining the flow of data between different components and services in a cloud infrastructure.

This process provides insights into how data moves within and across cloud environments, helping organizations identify anomalies and potential security threats.

One of the primary goals of cloud network traffic analysis is to ensure that data is flowing as expected and that there are no signs of unauthorized access or malicious activity.

It allows organizations to gain visibility into the traffic patterns and behaviors of their cloud resources, making it easier to detect and respond to security incidents.

In a cloud environment, network traffic can be generated by various sources, including virtual machines, containers, and serverless functions.

These resources communicate with each other and external services over the network, and monitoring this traffic is crucial for maintaining the integrity of cloud-based applications and data.

Cloud network traffic analysis tools and solutions use various techniques to capture and analyze network data.

One common method is packet capture, where network packets are intercepted and recorded for later analysis.

Packet capture provides detailed information about the content and behavior of network traffic, making it a valuable tool for security investigations.

Another approach is flow-based analysis, which focuses on aggregating and summarizing network flows to identify trends and anomalies.

Flow-based analysis is less resource-intensive than packet capture and can provide valuable insights into overall network activity.

Cloud network traffic analysis can be used for a variety of purposes, including security monitoring, performance optimization, and compliance auditing.

When it comes to security monitoring, cloud network traffic analysis helps organizations detect and respond to threats in real-time.

By analyzing network traffic patterns and identifying deviations from the norm, security teams can quickly identify potential security incidents and take appropriate action.

For example, if unusual outbound traffic is detected from a cloud server, it may indicate a compromised system attempting to communicate with a command and control server.

In such cases, immediate action can be taken to isolate the compromised resource and investigate the incident further.

Performance optimization is another critical use case for cloud network traffic analysis.

By monitoring network traffic, organizations can identify bottlenecks, latency issues, and other performance-related problems that may impact the user experience.

With this information, cloud administrators can make informed decisions about resource allocation and network configuration to improve application performance.

Additionally, cloud network traffic analysis can help organizations meet compliance requirements by providing detailed logs and reports on network activity.

This information can be invaluable during audits, as it demonstrates that security and data protection measures are in place and effective.

For example, organizations subject to data privacy regulations may need to show that they are encrypting sensitive data in transit.

Cloud network traffic analysis can generate reports that confirm the use of encryption protocols and demonstrate compliance.

To effectively perform cloud network traffic analysis, organizations need the right tools and technologies.

Many cloud providers offer built-in network monitoring and analysis features that can be leveraged to gain insights into network traffic within their respective environments.

These tools often provide dashboards and alerts that make it easier to identify and respond to security and performance issues.

However, for organizations with multi-cloud or hybrid cloud environments, a more comprehensive approach may be necessary.

Third-party network traffic analysis solutions can provide centralized visibility across multiple cloud providers and on-premises infrastructure.

These solutions typically offer advanced features such as machine learning-based anomaly detection and customizable dashboards.

When implementing cloud network traffic analysis, it's essential to define clear objectives and use cases.

Organizations should determine what they want to achieve through network traffic analysis, whether it's improving security, optimizing performance, or ensuring compliance.

Once objectives are defined, organizations can select the most appropriate tools and techniques to meet their needs.

It's also essential to establish baseline network traffic patterns and behaviors to help identify anomalies accurately.

This baseline can be used as a reference point for detecting deviations that may indicate security incidents or performance issues.

Regularly reviewing and updating network traffic analysis strategies is essential, as cloud environments are dynamic and constantly evolving.

New applications, services, and infrastructure changes can impact network traffic patterns, and organizations must adapt their analysis methods accordingly.

In summary, cloud network traffic analysis is a critical aspect of managing and securing cloud environments.

It provides visibility into the flow of data, helping organizations detect and respond to security threats, optimize performance, and ensure compliance with regulatory requirements.

By understanding the principles and tools of cloud network traffic analysis, organizations can effectively monitor and protect their cloud resources and data.

Cloud-specific network forensics tools are a crucial component of modern digital investigations.

These specialized tools are designed to analyze network traffic and activities in cloud environments, providing valuable insights into security incidents, data breaches, and other cyber threats.

As organizations increasingly migrate their IT infrastructure and services to the cloud, it has become essential to have dedicated tools for investigating network-related incidents in these environments.

Unlike traditional on-premises network forensics, cloud-specific tools are tailored to work seamlessly with cloud platforms and services, ensuring accurate and comprehensive analysis.

One of the primary functions of cloud-specific network forensics tools is the collection of network traffic data within a cloud environment.

These tools capture packets, logs, and other network-related information from various cloud resources, including virtual machines, containers, and serverless applications.

By collecting this data, investigators can reconstruct network sessions, identify communication patterns, and pinpoint potential security issues.

Cloud-specific network forensics tools support various cloud platforms, including Amazon Web Services (AWS), Microsoft Azure, and Google Cloud Platform (GCP).

They integrate with cloud-native services and APIs to gather data effectively and provide a unified view of network activity across multiple cloud providers.

Once network traffic data is collected, these tools offer advanced analysis capabilities to detect and investigate suspicious activities.

One crucial aspect of network forensics is the ability to identify security incidents promptly.

Cloud-specific tools use techniques such as packet inspection, flow analysis, and behavioral analytics to detect anomalies and potential threats.

For example, if there is a sudden spike in outbound traffic from a specific virtual machine in a cloud environment, it may indicate a compromised system attempting to exfiltrate data.

The tool can generate alerts for such anomalies, enabling security teams to respond quickly and mitigate potential damage.

Furthermore, cloud-specific network forensics tools assist investigators in visualizing network activity through interactive dashboards and reports. These visual representations help analysts understand the flow of data and communication patterns, making it easier to spot irregularities. In addition to identifying security incidents, these tools play a crucial role in post-incident investigations.

When a security breach or data breach occurs, investigators need to understand how the attack happened, what data was compromised, and the extent of the damage.

Cloud-specific network forensics tools provide detailed logs and historical data, allowing investigators to trace the attack's progression, from initial intrusion to data exfiltration. This information is invaluable for understanding the attacker's tactics, techniques, and procedures (TTPs) and strengthening the organization's security posture.

One of the advantages of cloud-specific network forensics tools is their ability to support multi-cloud and hybrid cloud environments. Many organizations use a combination of cloud providers and on-premises resources, making it challenging to investigate network incidents consistently.

These tools offer centralized management and analysis capabilities, allowing investigators to monitor network activity across various cloud platforms and infrastructure types. As organizations rely on cloud-based applications and services, it's essential to have the means to investigate incidents involving these resources.

Cloud-specific network forensics tools support the analysis of traffic within cloud applications and services, including web applications, databases, and storage services.

This capability helps organizations understand how data is accessed and manipulated within their cloud-based assets.

For example, if unauthorized access to a database in AWS is suspected, a cloud-specific network forensics tool can help investigators trace the source of the access and identify the activities performed.

Furthermore, these tools are designed to ensure data privacy and compliance with regulatory requirements.

When conducting network forensics investigations in the cloud, sensitive data may be involved.

Cloud-specific tools provide features for redacting or masking sensitive information in network traffic data, ensuring that privacy and compliance standards are maintained.

This is particularly crucial in industries with strict data protection regulations, such as healthcare and finance.

Another key aspect of cloud-specific network forensics tools is their integration with other security and incident response solutions.

They can share data and alerts with security information and event management (SIEM) systems, endpoint detection and response (EDR) solutions, and threat intelligence platforms.

This integration helps organizations correlate network data with other security events and indicators, improving their ability to detect and respond to threats effectively.

In summary, cloud-specific network forensics tools are indispensable for investigating network-related incidents in cloud environments.

These tools provide the means to collect, analyze, and visualize network traffic data, enabling organizations to detect and respond to security threats promptly.

They are essential for understanding the scope and impact of security incidents and for maintaining data privacy and compliance in the cloud.

As organizations continue to embrace cloud technologies, the use of cloud-specific network forensics tools will become increasingly critical in maintaining the security and integrity of cloud-based resources.

Chapter 9: Legal and Ethical Considerations in Cloud Forensics

The admissibility of cloud evidence in court is a topic of growing importance in the digital age.

Courts are increasingly dealing with cases that involve evidence stored in the cloud, such as emails, documents, and digital communications.

However, the admissibility of this evidence can be subject to legal challenges and requirements that vary by jurisdiction.

In many legal systems, the admissibility of evidence is governed by rules and standards that have evolved over centuries.

These rules are designed to ensure that evidence presented in court is reliable, relevant, and obtained legally.

When it comes to cloud evidence, several key considerations come into play.

One of the primary concerns is the authentication of cloud-based evidence.

Courts need to establish that the evidence is what it claims to be and that it has not been tampered with.

This can be challenging with cloud evidence, as it may involve data stored on remote servers owned and controlled by third-party providers.

To address this issue, parties seeking to introduce cloud evidence must often demonstrate its authenticity.

This may involve providing documentation from the cloud service provider, such as records of account access or data transfer logs.

Additionally, digital signatures, metadata, and encryption can all play a role in authenticating cloud evidence.

Another critical consideration is the chain of custody for cloud evidence.

The chain of custody refers to the documented trail that shows how evidence was collected, handled, and preserved from the moment it was discovered to the moment it is presented in court.

Maintaining a proper chain of custody is essential to establish that the evidence has not been tampered with or altered.

With cloud evidence, establishing a chain of custody can be complex, especially when data is stored remotely and accessed through the internet.

Digital forensics experts often play a crucial role in documenting the chain of custody for cloud evidence, ensuring its integrity and admissibility.

Privacy and data protection laws can also impact the admissibility of cloud evidence in court.

Many countries have strict regulations governing the collection and sharing of personal data, and cloud evidence often contains sensitive information.

Courts must consider whether the collection and use of cloud evidence comply with applicable data protection laws.

For example, in the European Union, the General Data Protection Regulation (GDPR) imposes strict requirements on the processing of personal data, including evidence collection.

To ensure admissibility, parties may need to redact or anonymize sensitive information in cloud evidence or obtain consent from data subjects.

Furthermore, the location of cloud servers can be a factor in determining the admissibility of evidence.

Some countries have specific requirements regarding the storage and transfer of data outside their borders.

Cloud evidence stored on servers located in foreign countries may raise jurisdictional and legal issues.

Parties seeking to introduce such evidence may need to demonstrate that it complies with applicable laws and regulations.

In some cases, courts may require legal assistance treaties or other forms of cooperation between countries to obtain cloud evidence stored abroad.

Additionally, the reliability of cloud evidence can be a subject of scrutiny in court.

This includes assessing the accuracy and trustworthiness of the data presented.

Courts may consider factors such as the security measures employed by the cloud service provider, the integrity of data transmission, and the reliability of digital records.

Parties may need to provide expert testimony to establish the reliability of cloud evidence and address any doubts or challenges raised by opposing parties.

Ultimately, the admissibility of cloud evidence in court depends on various factors, including legal standards, jurisdictional considerations, and the specific circumstances of the case.

Courts must weigh these factors to determine whether the evidence is admissible and relevant to the case.

As cloud technology continues to evolve, so too will the legal standards and practices surrounding the use of cloud evidence in court.

Legal professionals, digital forensics experts, and cloud service providers all play essential roles in addressing the complex issues surrounding the admissibility of cloud evidence and ensuring that justice is served in the digital age.

Privacy and ethical considerations are of paramount

importance in the realm of cloud investigations, where digital forensics professionals navigate a complex landscape of data access, collection, and analysis.

In an era where vast amounts of personal and sensitive information are stored in cloud environments, respecting individual privacy rights is a fundamental ethical principle.

Balancing the pursuit of justice with the preservation of privacy is a delicate task that digital forensics experts must tackle.

One of the primary ethical concerns in cloud investigations is the potential invasion of privacy.

Individuals and organizations trust cloud service providers with their data, expecting it to be stored securely and accessed only under specific circumstances.

When conducting investigations, it is crucial to respect these expectations and legal requirements.

Accessing cloud data without proper authorization or consent can raise significant privacy concerns and may even violate data protection laws.

Digital forensics professionals must carefully navigate these issues, ensuring that their actions are legal and ethical.

Transparency is a key element in addressing privacy concerns during cloud investigations.

This entails clearly communicating the scope and purpose of the investigation to all relevant parties.

Informing individuals about the collection and use of their data is not only an ethical responsibility but also a legal requirement in many jurisdictions.

Consent plays a pivotal role in respecting privacy rights.

Obtaining informed consent from data subjects before accessing their cloud data is a best practice that helps ensure the ethical conduct of investigations.

However, there are situations where consent may not be feasible, such as in criminal investigations or cases involving emergency data access.

In such instances, legal processes and warrants may be necessary to access cloud data, but these should be pursued with strict adherence to the law and ethical principles.

Another ethical consideration is the principle of proportionality.

This means that the scope and depth of data collection and analysis should be proportional to the objectives of the investigation.

Overzealous or indiscriminate data collection can infringe on privacy rights and should be avoided.

Instead, investigators should focus on collecting only the data that is directly relevant to the case at hand.

The retention and handling of data also pose ethical dilemmas.

Digital forensics professionals must establish proper procedures for data storage and disposal to ensure that sensitive information is adequately protected.

This includes securely erasing data when it is no longer needed for the investigation and taking measures to prevent data breaches or leaks.

Furthermore, respecting attorney-client privilege and other legally recognized privileges is an ethical imperative.

Investigators should not access or disclose privileged communications, as doing so would violate ethical and legal standards.

Cloud investigations often involve multinational or cross-border considerations, which add complexity to privacy and ethical concerns.

Different countries have varying laws and regulations governing data privacy, and these must be navigated carefully to ensure ethical conduct.

Legal professionals and digital forensics experts must work collaboratively to address these challenges and ensure that investigations comply with applicable laws and ethical standards.

Moreover, the use of encryption and other security measures in cloud environments introduces ethical considerations.

Attempting to circumvent encryption or compromise the security of cloud data may raise ethical red flags.

Balancing the need to access data for legitimate investigative purposes with the duty to maintain data security is a delicate ethical balancing act.

Transparency, accountability, and adherence to legal and ethical principles are essential in this regard.

Ethical considerations also extend to the use of cloud-based evidence in legal proceedings.

Digital forensics professionals must ensure that the evidence they present in court is not only legally admissible but also ethically obtained.

This includes providing clear documentation of how the evidence was collected, handled, and analyzed, as well as any ethical considerations that were taken into account.

In summary, privacy and ethical considerations are integral components of cloud investigations.

Respecting individual privacy rights, obtaining informed consent, adhering to legal standards, and maintaining transparency and accountability are all essential ethical principles that guide the actions of digital forensics professionals in this complex field.

Balancing the pursuit of justice with the preservation of privacy is a challenging but necessary endeavor in the world of cloud investigations.

Chapter 10: Case Studies and Lessons Learned

In the ever-evolving landscape of cloud computing, real-world security incidents serve as invaluable case studies and cautionary tales.

These incidents provide practical insights into the vulnerabilities and threats that organizations face when adopting cloud technologies.

One such incident that garnered significant attention was the Capital One data breach in 2019.

In this high-profile case, a former employee of a cloud service provider exploited a misconfiguration in a web application firewall to gain unauthorized access to sensitive customer data stored on Amazon Web Services (AWS).

The breach exposed the personal and financial information of over 100 million customers and highlighted the importance of robust security controls and monitoring in the cloud.

Another noteworthy incident involved the healthcare organization Quest Diagnostics in 2019.

A third-party billing collections vendor experienced a data breach that exposed the personal and medical information of nearly 12 million patients.

This incident underscored the need for organizations to thoroughly vet and monitor the security practices of their cloud service providers and third-party partners.

In 2020, a series of ransomware attacks targeting healthcare institutions in the United States disrupted critical services and compromised patient records.

These incidents emphasized the critical importance of data backup and recovery strategies in the cloud, as well as the need for proactive threat detection and response measures.

In the financial sector, the 2020 attack on Blackbaud, a provider of cloud-based fundraising and financial management software, highlighted the risk of cybercriminals targeting cloud service providers to gain access to sensitive customer data.

Incidents like these underscore the shared responsibility model in cloud security, where both the cloud provider and the customer have distinct roles in securing data and systems.

In 2021, a significant cloud security incident involved the Conti ransomware group targeting a major U.S. pipeline operator, Colonial Pipeline.

The attack disrupted the flow of fuel along the East Coast, resulting in fuel shortages and highlighting the potential for cyberattacks on critical infrastructure that relies on cloud-based systems.

These real-world incidents demonstrate that cloud security is an ongoing challenge that requires a holistic approach.

Organizations must adopt a multi-layered defense strategy that includes proactive threat detection, encryption, access controls, and incident response plans.

Another aspect of cloud security incidents involves accidental data exposure.

In 2020, researchers discovered that millions of sensitive files, including personal photographs and medical records, were publicly accessible due to misconfigured cloud storage buckets.

These incidents underscore the importance of proper cloud configuration management and ongoing monitoring to prevent inadvertent data exposure.

In addition to external threats, insider threats remain a significant concern in cloud security.

Incidents involving malicious or negligent employees or contractors can lead to data breaches and financial losses.

One prominent example is the case of an ex-employee of Tesla who allegedly attempted to sabotage the company's operations by accessing and disseminating confidential information stored in the cloud.

This incident highlights the need for robust identity and access management (IAM) controls and privileged access monitoring.

Moreover, cloud-based email platforms have become a common target for phishing attacks, where cybercriminals attempt to trick users into revealing sensitive information.

For instance, the SolarWinds supply chain attack in 2020 began with a phishing campaign that targeted employees of a cloud email provider.

As a result, it is crucial for organizations to invest in user education and email security solutions to mitigate these threats.

The impact of cloud security incidents extends beyond financial losses and data exposure.

Reputation damage, legal ramifications, and regulatory fines can all result from a security breach.

For example, the European Union's General Data Protection Regulation (GDPR) imposes hefty fines on organizations that fail to protect the personal data of EU residents.

Cloud security incidents that lead to data breaches can trigger GDPR violations and penalties.

To mitigate these risks, organizations must prioritize compliance with data protection regulations and implement robust data governance practices in the cloud.

In summary, real-world cloud security incidents serve as powerful reminders of the evolving threat landscape and the critical importance of cloud security.

From data breaches and ransomware attacks to accidental data exposure and insider threats, these incidents highlight the need for comprehensive security strategies, proactive monitoring, and ongoing vigilance in the cloud.

By learning from these incidents and adopting best practices, organizations can better protect their data and systems in an increasingly digital and interconnected world.

Key takeaways and best practices gleaned from the analysis of real-world case studies in cloud security provide invaluable insights into protecting your organization's digital assets in an ever-evolving threat landscape.

One crucial lesson is the importance of thorough and ongoing security training and awareness programs for all employees and contractors.

These programs can help individuals recognize phishing attempts, avoid social engineering tactics, and understand their roles and responsibilities in safeguarding sensitive data.

Another key takeaway is the significance of strong access control measures, including multifactor authentication (MFA) and role-based access control (RBAC).

Implementing these measures can reduce the risk of unauthorized access and privilege escalation, as demonstrated in several case studies where insider threats exploited weak access controls.

Additionally, continuous monitoring and auditing of user activities and system logs are essential.

Case studies have shown that early detection of anomalous behavior and rapid incident response can significantly mitigate the impact of security incidents.

A proactive approach to security, including regular vulnerability assessments and penetration testing, can help identify and remediate weaknesses in your cloud infrastructure before attackers can exploit them.

Moreover, encryption plays a critical role in protecting data both in transit and at rest.

Many case studies highlight the significance of encrypting sensitive information to prevent unauthorized access, even if a breach occurs.

Regularly updating and patching cloud resources is a fundamental practice that can prevent known vulnerabilities from being exploited.

Failing to apply security patches promptly has led to numerous security incidents, underscoring the importance of patch management.

Furthermore, organizations should establish an incident response plan that outlines the steps to take when a security incident occurs.

Case studies have revealed that a well-defined and rehearsed incident response plan can minimize downtime and data exposure during a breach.

Backups and disaster recovery plans are essential components of cloud security.

Several incidents have resulted in data loss or unavailability, emphasizing the need for regular backups and a robust recovery strategy.

Cloud providers offer various security tools and services that organizations can leverage to enhance their security posture.

These include identity and access management (IAM) services, security information and event management (SIEM) solutions, and threat detection tools.

Collaboration with cloud providers can help organizations take advantage of these offerings and strengthen their security.

Another takeaway from case studies is the importance of transparency and communication during and after a security incident.

Organizations should be prepared to communicate with affected parties, such as customers and regulatory authorities, promptly and honestly.

Privacy and compliance regulations, such as the General Data Protection Regulation (GDPR) and the Health Insurance Portability and Accountability Act (HIPAA), have legal requirements for reporting data breaches.

Organizations must be aware of these regulations and ensure compliance when handling security incidents.

In summary, real-world case studies in cloud security provide valuable lessons and best practices for organizations seeking to protect their digital assets.

From user training and access controls to encryption, monitoring, and incident response planning, these case studies underscore the multifaceted nature of cloud security.

By incorporating these key takeaways and best practices into their security strategies, organizations can better defend against a wide range of threats and ensure the safety of their data and systems.

BOOK 4
EXPERT CLOUD SECURITY AND COMPLIANCE AUTOMATION
AZURE, AWS, AND GCP BEST PRACTICES

ROB BOTWRIGHT

Chapter 1: Advanced Cloud Security and Compliance Landscape

In the fast-evolving landscape of cloud computing, staying ahead of emerging threats is paramount to maintaining a robust security posture. As organizations increasingly embrace advanced cloud environments, they find themselves facing new and complex challenges in protecting their digital assets.

One of the emerging threats in advanced cloud environments is the rise of sophisticated cyber-attacks, often driven by nation-state actors or organized cybercrime groups. These attackers employ highly advanced techniques, such as zero-day exploits and custom malware, to target cloud infrastructure.

Moreover, supply chain attacks have become a growing concern in the cloud ecosystem. Attackers may compromise third-party software or services integrated into a cloud environment, enabling them to infiltrate the organization's systems through trusted channels.

Another significant concern is the increasing use of artificial intelligence (AI) and machine learning (ML) by cybercriminals. These technologies can be weaponized to automate attacks, adapt to security defenses, and rapidly identify vulnerabilities.

In advanced cloud environments, the attack surface is often broader and more complex than in traditional on-premises setups. The deployment of microservices, serverless computing, and containerization introduces additional potential entry points for attackers.

As cloud environments become more distributed and interconnected, the threat of lateral movement within cloud networks becomes more pronounced. Attackers who gain initial access may attempt to move laterally to compromise other resources and data.

Furthermore, the insider threat remains a persistent concern in advanced cloud settings. Insiders with privileged access can cause significant damage, whether intentionally or unintentionally, by misconfiguring cloud resources or exfiltrating sensitive data.

The use of cloud-native technologies and services also introduces novel security challenges. Serverless computing, for example, relies on ephemeral functions, making traditional security controls less effective.

The adoption of multi-cloud and hybrid cloud architectures complicates security management. Organizations must ensure consistent security policies and monitoring across diverse cloud providers and on-premises infrastructure.

Additionally, compliance and regulatory requirements continue to evolve, adding complexity to the security landscape. Organizations operating in multiple regions or industries may face varying compliance mandates that must be addressed within their cloud environments.

One emerging threat that has gained prominence is the exploitation of misconfigured cloud resources. Security misconfigurations can expose sensitive data or grant unauthorized access to attackers. Addressing these issues requires rigorous configuration management and regular audits.

In advanced cloud environments, the visibility and control of network traffic become more challenging. Attackers may leverage encrypted traffic to hide their activities, making it essential for organizations to implement effective network monitoring and threat detection solutions.

As cloud environments scale and become more dynamic, managing identities and access becomes increasingly complex. Ensuring the right individuals have the appropriate level of access, without granting excessive privileges, is an ongoing challenge.

Advanced threat actors often employ techniques such as cloud-specific phishing campaigns or social engineering to target cloud administrators and gain unauthorized access. Educating users and administrators about these threats is crucial.

In response to these emerging threats, organizations must adopt a proactive and adaptive security approach. Threat intelligence and real-time monitoring are essential for identifying and responding to novel attack vectors promptly.

Security teams should leverage advanced security analytics and AI-driven tools to detect suspicious activities and anomalies in real-time. These technologies can help organizations stay ahead of threat actors by identifying patterns and behaviors indicative of an attack.

Additionally, organizations should conduct regular red team exercises and penetration testing to assess their readiness and resilience against emerging threats. These exercises allow security teams to identify vulnerabilities and weaknesses before malicious actors can exploit them.

Collaboration and information sharing within the cloud security community are vital in staying informed about emerging threats and best practices. Security professionals should actively participate in industry forums, conferences, and threat intelligence sharing initiatives.

In summary, as advanced cloud environments become the norm, organizations face a shifting threat landscape that demands constant vigilance and adaptation. Emerging threats driven by sophisticated attackers, supply chain vulnerabilities, AI-powered attacks, and insider threats all require careful consideration and proactive security measures.

To protect their cloud assets effectively, organizations must prioritize threat intelligence, real-time monitoring, adaptive security strategies, and ongoing education and training for their teams. By staying informed, proactive, and collaborative, organizations can navigate the challenges of advanced cloud security and safeguard their digital future.

Navigating the complex landscape of regulatory requirements is an ongoing challenge for organizations operating in the cloud, and these requirements continue to evolve.

Regulatory compliance has always been a crucial aspect of maintaining trust and integrity in the cloud, but it has become even more intricate in recent years.

One of the primary reasons for this complexity is the global nature of cloud computing. Organizations often operate across borders, making them subject to multiple sets of regulations, each with its own unique demands.

In the European Union, for instance, the General Data Protection Regulation (GDPR) has had a significant impact on how organizations handle personal data. GDPR's strict requirements for data protection, consent, and breach reporting have forced many organizations to reevaluate their data management practices.

In the United States, various state-level regulations, such as the California Consumer Privacy Act (CCPA) and the New York Shield Act, have introduced additional layers of complexity to cloud compliance. Organizations must navigate a patchwork of state laws while also adhering to federal regulations like the Health Insurance Portability and Accountability Act (HIPAA) and the Gramm-Leach-Bliley Act (GLBA).

Furthermore, cloud compliance extends beyond geographical borders. Organizations must consider industry-specific regulations, such as the Payment Card Industry Data Security Standard (PCI DSS) for businesses that handle credit card data.

The rapid pace of technological innovation and the growing reliance on cloud services have made it challenging for regulatory bodies to keep up. As a result, regulations are continually evolving to address new security threats and data privacy concerns.

For example, in response to the increasing prevalence of data breaches, many regulations now require organizations to implement robust incident response and breach notification procedures. This places an additional burden on organizations to proactively prepare for security incidents and ensure compliance with notification timelines.

Cloud service providers also play a role in compliance. Leading cloud providers like AWS, Azure, and GCP offer compliance certifications and services to help organizations meet specific regulatory requirements. However, it remains the responsibility of the organization to configure and use these services correctly.

The advent of multi-cloud and hybrid cloud environments has introduced new challenges in cloud compliance. Organizations must ensure that their data and operations comply with regulations, regardless of the cloud providers they use. This requires consistent policies, monitoring, and reporting across different cloud platforms.

Another emerging trend is the growing emphasis on supply chain security. Regulatory bodies are increasingly focused on ensuring that organizations secure their supply chains, as third-party vulnerabilities can lead to significant security breaches. This places additional scrutiny on organizations' vendor management practices and requires them to assess and manage the security of their cloud service providers.

To address these evolving regulatory requirements, organizations must adopt a proactive and holistic approach to cloud compliance. This includes regularly reviewing and updating their compliance policies, conducting risk assessments, and implementing security controls to protect sensitive data.

Additionally, organizations should invest in employee training and awareness programs to ensure that all staff members understand their roles and responsibilities in maintaining compliance. This includes data handling, incident reporting, and privacy protection.

Automation can also be a valuable tool in maintaining compliance. By automating compliance checks and reporting, organizations can streamline the process of demonstrating adherence to regulatory requirements.

Collaboration and information sharing with industry peers can be beneficial in staying informed about evolving regulatory requirements and best practices. Industry forums and associations often provide valuable insights and resources for addressing compliance challenges.

In summary, as cloud computing continues to reshape the digital landscape, regulatory requirements in cloud compliance will continue to evolve. Organizations must stay informed about these changes, adapt their policies and practices accordingly, and foster a culture of compliance within their teams. By doing so, they can navigate the complex regulatory landscape and ensure that their cloud operations meet the highest standards of security and data protection.

Chapter 2: Cloud Security Automation Frameworks

In the ever-evolving landscape of cybersecurity, organizations are facing increasingly sophisticated threats that require swift and effective responses.

Security automation frameworks have emerged as a critical component in enhancing an organization's ability to detect, respond to, and mitigate security incidents.

These frameworks are designed to streamline security operations, reduce response times, and improve overall incident management.

At their core, security automation frameworks leverage technology to automate repetitive and time-consuming security tasks.

By automating these tasks, organizations can free up their cybersecurity teams to focus on more complex and strategic aspects of security.

One of the primary goals of security automation frameworks is to improve an organization's ability to detect security incidents in real-time or near-real-time.

This is achieved through the integration of various security tools and systems, such as intrusion detection systems (IDS), security information and event management (SIEM) solutions, and threat intelligence feeds.

When an incident is detected, the framework can automatically trigger predefined response actions, such as isolating a compromised system, blocking malicious traffic, or alerting security personnel.

These automated responses help organizations reduce the "dwell time" of attackers within their networks, limiting the potential damage they can cause.

In addition to incident detection and response, security automation frameworks can also assist organizations in other critical areas, such as vulnerability management and compliance.

For example, these frameworks can automate vulnerability scans, prioritize remediation efforts, and even apply patches or configuration changes automatically.

This not only improves an organization's overall security posture but also helps maintain compliance with regulatory requirements and industry standards.

Furthermore, security automation frameworks can enhance an organization's ability to orchestrate and coordinate incident response activities.

By defining and automating workflows, these frameworks ensure that the right people are notified, the right actions are taken, and the right information is shared during an incident.

This level of coordination is essential for effective incident response, especially in large and complex organizations.

Another important aspect of security automation frameworks is their ability to facilitate threat intelligence sharing and collaboration.

These frameworks can ingest threat intelligence feeds from various sources, such as government agencies, industry information sharing and analysis centers (ISACs), and commercial threat intelligence providers.

The intelligence is then correlated with the organization's own security data to identify potential threats and vulnerabilities.

This proactive approach allows organizations to stay ahead of emerging threats and adapt their defenses accordingly.

The benefits of security automation frameworks are numerous, but it's important to acknowledge that implementing them effectively can be a challenging endeavor.

Organizations must carefully plan and design their automation processes to ensure that they align with their specific security goals and requirements.

Additionally, they must invest in the necessary technology and infrastructure to support automation.

This may include selecting and integrating security tools that are compatible with the chosen framework and ensuring that data sources are accessible and properly configured.

Moreover, organizations should establish clear policies and procedures for security automation to avoid unintended consequences or security incidents caused by misconfigurations.

Training and skill development are also essential for security teams to fully leverage the capabilities of automation frameworks.

As these frameworks continue to evolve, organizations can expect to see more advanced features and capabilities.

Machine learning and artificial intelligence are being integrated into these frameworks to enhance threat detection and response.

For example, machine learning algorithms can analyze large volumes of security data to identify anomalous behavior patterns that may indicate a security incident.

As automation becomes more sophisticated, organizations will also need to consider ethical and legal implications.

For instance, decisions made by automated systems, such as blocking a network connection or quarantining a system, may have legal consequences, and organizations should be prepared to address these issues.

In summary, security automation frameworks play a vital role in modern cybersecurity by improving incident detection and response, streamlining security operations, and enhancing overall security posture.

These frameworks offer organizations the opportunity to leverage technology and automation to stay ahead of evolving threats and ensure a proactive and coordinated approach to security.

While implementing security automation frameworks can be challenging, the benefits far outweigh the effort, making them an essential component of any robust cybersecurity strategy.

Implementing security policies with automation is a crucial strategy for organizations seeking to enhance their cybersecurity posture.

Security policies serve as a set of guidelines and rules that dictate how an organization should protect its information, systems, and networks.

These policies help define acceptable behavior, establish best practices, and ensure compliance with regulatory requirements and industry standards.

However, enforcing these policies manually can be a daunting and error-prone task, especially in large and complex environments.

This is where automation comes into play, providing organizations with the means to implement, monitor, and enforce security policies consistently and efficiently.

One of the primary benefits of implementing security policies with automation is the reduction of human error.

Manual enforcement of policies often relies on individuals to configure and manage security controls, leaving room for misconfigurations or omissions.

Automation, on the other hand, can ensure that policies are applied consistently across all relevant systems and devices.

This reduces the risk of misconfigurations and enhances the overall security of the organization.

Automation can also significantly improve the speed and agility of policy enforcement.

In today's dynamic threat landscape, organizations need to respond rapidly to emerging threats and vulnerabilities.

With automation, security policies can be enforced in real-time or near-real-time, allowing organizations to mitigate risks and vulnerabilities more quickly.

For example, automated tools can detect and respond to suspicious network traffic, block malicious IP addresses, or apply security patches as soon as they become available.

Moreover, automation can help organizations achieve continuous compliance with various regulations and standards.

Maintaining compliance is a complex and ongoing process that requires regular assessments, audits, and adjustments to security controls.

By automating compliance checks and reporting, organizations can streamline these activities and ensure that they are always in line with the latest requirements.

Another advantage of implementing security policies with automation is the ability to scale security operations effectively.

As organizations grow and their IT environments become more diverse, manual policy enforcement becomes increasingly challenging.

Automation allows organizations to manage and monitor security policies across a wide range of devices, applications, and cloud services without significantly increasing the workload of their security teams.

Furthermore, automation can enhance threat detection and response capabilities by integrating security information and event management (SIEM) systems with other security tools.

This enables organizations to correlate and analyze vast amounts of security data in real-time, identify potential threats, and trigger automated responses when suspicious activities are detected.

For instance, if an SIEM system identifies a series of failed login attempts on a critical system, it can automatically block the source IP address and alert the security team.

Implementing security policies with automation also facilitates incident response by enabling organizations to orchestrate and coordinate response actions.

When a security incident occurs, automation can ensure that the right people are notified, the affected systems are isolated, and the incident is thoroughly investigated.

This level of coordination is crucial for minimizing the impact of security incidents and reducing downtime.

However, implementing security policies with automation requires careful planning and consideration.

Organizations must define clear objectives and requirements for their automation initiatives.

They need to identify the security policies that can be automated, the tools and technologies required, and the workflows for policy enforcement and incident response.

Additionally, organizations must ensure that their automation processes align with their overall security strategy and risk management approach.

Furthermore, it's essential to regularly review and update automated security policies to reflect changes in the threat landscape, regulatory requirements, and organizational priorities.

In summary, implementing security policies with automation is a powerful strategy for organizations seeking to enhance their cybersecurity defenses.

Automation can reduce human error, improve the speed and agility of policy enforcement, enable continuous compliance, and enhance threat detection and response capabilities. However, it requires careful planning and consideration to ensure that it aligns with an organization's specific security objectives and risk management approach.

Chapter 3: Infrastructure as Code (IaC) for Security

Security considerations in Infrastructure as Code (IaC) are of paramount importance in today's cloud-centric IT landscape. IaC refers to the practice of managing and provisioning infrastructure using code and automation rather than manual processes.

While IaC offers numerous benefits, such as increased agility and scalability, it also introduces new security challenges that organizations must address.

One of the fundamental security considerations in IaC is ensuring the integrity and security of the code itself.

The code used to define infrastructure resources, such as virtual machines, networks, and storage, should be subject to rigorous code review and testing to identify vulnerabilities and misconfigurations.

Furthermore, organizations should follow best practices for secure coding to minimize the risk of introducing security flaws in their IaC templates.

Another key security aspect of IaC is the management of secrets and sensitive data.

In many IaC templates, credentials, access keys, and other sensitive information may be required to configure and provision resources.

It's critical to secure these secrets and ensure that they are not exposed in plain text within the code or stored in insecure locations.

Organizations should leverage secret management tools and practices to store, retrieve, and use secrets securely in IaC templates.

Access control is another vital security consideration in IaC.

Access permissions to IaC templates and the infrastructure they define should be strictly controlled and limited to authorized personnel.

Role-Based Access Control (RBAC) should be used to assign appropriate permissions, and multifactor authentication (MFA) should be enforced for accessing IaC repositories and automation tools.

Moreover, organizations should implement auditing and monitoring of IaC activities to detect and respond to any unauthorized changes or access.

Regularly reviewing access logs and monitoring for suspicious activities can help organizations maintain a strong security posture.

One of the strengths of IaC is the ability to version and track changes to infrastructure configurations over time.

However, this also means that any security misconfigurations or vulnerabilities introduced into the code can persist and be propagated if not detected and remediated promptly.

Continuous security scanning and vulnerability assessments of IaC templates are crucial to identifying and addressing security issues as soon as they arise.

Automation tools can assist in this process by integrating security checks into the development pipeline.

It's essential to maintain an up-to-date inventory of IaC templates and their dependencies to ensure that all code is scanned and assessed for vulnerabilities.

Moreover, organizations should consider implementing automated testing and validation of IaC templates to ensure that they adhere to security best practices and compliance requirements.

Secure parameterization is another essential aspect of IaC security.

This involves parameterizing IaC templates to allow dynamic configuration without hardcoding sensitive information.

By parameterizing sensitive values, such as passwords or API keys, organizations can reduce the risk of exposure and enable more flexible and secure deployments.

Encryption plays a significant role in securing IaC workflows.

Data at rest and in transit should be encrypted to protect it from unauthorized access or interception.

Organizations should use encryption mechanisms, such as SSL/TLS for data in transit and encryption at rest for data stored in IaC repositories or configuration files.

Furthermore, encryption keys should be managed securely and rotated regularly.

Implementing a robust key management strategy is crucial to maintaining the confidentiality and integrity of encrypted data.

Infrastructure as Code also raises concerns about the secure distribution and storage of code and configuration files.

Organizations should choose secure and reputable version control systems and repositories to store their IaC code.

Access to these repositories should be protected, and strong authentication mechanisms should be enforced.

Moreover, organizations should maintain backup copies of their IaC code to mitigate the risk of data loss or corruption.

When it comes to IaC deployment, organizations should consider deploying resources in isolated network environments, such as Virtual Private Clouds (VPCs) or Virtual Networks.

This isolation can help limit the attack surface and reduce the risk of lateral movement by malicious actors.

Furthermore, implementing network security controls, such as firewalls and intrusion detection systems, can enhance the security of IaC deployments.

Security testing of IaC templates should be an integral part of the development and deployment process.

Automated security testing tools can identify vulnerabilities, misconfigurations, and compliance violations in IaC code.

Regularly scheduled security scans and assessments should be conducted to maintain a secure IaC environment.

Additionally, organizations should have incident response plans in place specifically tailored to IaC security incidents.

These plans should outline the steps to be taken in the event of a security breach or compromise of IaC code.

Moreover, organizations should conduct post-incident reviews to learn from security incidents and improve their IaC security practices.

It's essential to stay informed about emerging threats and vulnerabilities related to IaC.

Security researchers regularly discover new attack vectors and vulnerabilities that can affect IaC workflows.

Organizations should follow security news and updates to ensure that their security measures are up to date.

Furthermore, organizations should engage in threat modeling and risk assessments to identify potential security weaknesses in their IaC implementations.

Collaboration between development and security teams is critical in addressing security considerations in IaC effectively.

Security professionals should work closely with developers to embed security practices into the IaC development process.

Moreover, security training and awareness programs for development teams can help them understand and prioritize security in their work.

In summary, security considerations in Infrastructure as Code are crucial for maintaining a robust and resilient cloud infrastructure.

Organizations should prioritize code integrity, secure secrets management, access control, continuous security scanning, and encryption when implementing IaC workflows.

Additionally, they should have an incident response plan, stay informed about emerging threats, and foster collaboration between development and security teams to ensure the security of their IaC environments.

Secure coding practices for Infrastructure as Code (IaC) templates are essential to ensure the integrity, confidentiality, and availability of cloud resources.

When creating IaC templates, it's crucial to start with a solid foundation by selecting a reputable and well-maintained IaC framework or tool.

Popular choices include AWS CloudFormation, Azure Resource Manager templates, Terraform, and Google Cloud Deployment Manager.

These tools have built-in security features and are regularly updated to address vulnerabilities.

Once you've chosen your IaC tool, it's essential to follow security best practices from the beginning of your template development process.

First and foremost, avoid hardcoding sensitive information, such as credentials, access keys, or passwords, directly into your templates.

Instead, use secure parameterization to inject these values dynamically when deploying your infrastructure.

By parameterizing your templates, you reduce the risk of exposing sensitive information and make it easier to manage secrets securely.

To enhance security further, leverage secret management solutions, like HashiCorp Vault or AWS Secrets Manager, to store and retrieve sensitive data.

Implementing Role-Based Access Control (RBAC) is another critical secure coding practice for IaC.

RBAC allows you to define and manage who can access and modify your IaC templates and infrastructure.

Assign permissions based on job roles, responsibilities, and the principle of least privilege to limit access to only those who need it.

Additionally, consider enforcing multifactor authentication (MFA) for accessing your IaC repositories and automation tools to add an extra layer of security.

When writing your IaC templates, follow secure coding principles to minimize vulnerabilities and misconfigurations.

Avoid using hardcoded IP addresses, public access to resources, or overly permissive security groups or firewall rules.

Instead, use variables and parameters to configure these aspects dynamically, and employ the principle of least privilege to restrict access only to necessary entities.

Code reviews and security assessments should be an integral part of your secure coding practices for IaC.

Regularly review your IaC templates for security vulnerabilities and misconfigurations, and involve security experts in the process.

Automated security scanning tools can help identify common issues and ensure compliance with security standards.

Furthermore, establish a process for code review and validation before deploying changes to your cloud environment.

Documentation is often an overlooked aspect of secure coding for IaC templates, but it's crucial for maintaining security.

Document your templates thoroughly, explaining the purpose of each resource, the rationale behind security configurations, and any known security considerations.

This documentation not only helps your team understand the code but also aids in audits and compliance assessments.

One of the advantages of IaC is the ability to version and track changes to your infrastructure code.

However, this feature can also pose security risks if not managed properly.

Ensure that your code repositories are secure and that access is limited to authorized personnel.

Use strong authentication mechanisms and enforce access controls to protect your IaC code.

Additionally, regularly back up your code repositories to prevent data loss or corruption.

When deploying IaC templates, it's essential to consider network security.

Deploy resources within isolated network environments, such as Virtual Private Clouds (VPCs) or Virtual Networks, to limit the attack surface and reduce the risk of lateral movement.

Implement network security controls like firewalls, intrusion detection systems, and security groups to enhance your IaC deployments' security posture.

Encryption plays a significant role in securing IaC workflows.

Ensure that data at rest and in transit is encrypted to protect it from unauthorized access or interception.

Use SSL/TLS for data in transit and encryption at rest for data stored within IaC repositories or configuration files.

Implement a robust key management strategy to secure encryption keys and ensure they are rotated regularly.

Automation and orchestration are core aspects of IaC, and they can also be leveraged to enhance security.

Automate security checks and scans as part of your continuous integration and continuous delivery (CI/CD) pipeline.

Integrate security testing into your development process to identify vulnerabilities early and prevent them from being deployed into your cloud environment.

Maintaining an inventory of your IaC templates and their dependencies is crucial for security.

By knowing what templates are in use and which versions are deployed, you can respond quickly to security vulnerabilities or critical updates.

Regularly assess your IaC code for compliance with security standards and best practices.

Consider using automated testing and validation tools to ensure that your templates adhere to security guidelines and policies.

One often overlooked aspect of secure coding for IaC is incident response planning.

Have a well-defined incident response plan specifically tailored to IaC security incidents.

This plan should outline the steps to take in the event of a security breach or compromise of IaC code.

Additionally, conduct post-incident reviews to learn from security incidents and improve your IaC security practices.

Staying informed about emerging threats and vulnerabilities related to IaC is crucial.

Security researchers regularly discover new attack vectors and vulnerabilities that can impact IaC workflows.

Subscribe to security news and updates to ensure that your security measures are up-to-date.

Engage in threat modeling and risk assessments to identify potential threats and prioritize security efforts accordingly.

Lastly, foster a culture of security within your development and operations teams.

Security is a shared responsibility, and everyone involved in the IaC process should be aware of security best practices.

Provide security training and awareness programs to educate your team members about secure coding practices and potential threats.

Encourage open communication and collaboration between development and security teams to address security concerns effectively.

In summary, secure coding practices for Infrastructure as Code (IaC) templates are essential for maintaining the security of your cloud infrastructure.

Start by selecting a reputable IaC framework or tool and avoid hardcoding sensitive information.

Implement Role-Based Access Control (RBAC), follow secure coding principles, and conduct code reviews and security assessments regularly.

Document your templates, secure your code repositories, and consider network security, encryption, and automation in your IaC workflows.

Maintain an inventory of your templates, have an incident response plan, and stay informed about emerging threats.

Finally, foster a culture of security within your organization to ensure that security is everyone's responsibility.

Chapter 4: Advanced Identity and Access Management Automation

Advanced Identity and Access Management (IAM) policies and role assignments are pivotal in controlling access to cloud resources with precision and granularity.

IAM policies serve as the blueprint for specifying who can do what in your cloud environment, offering a fine-tuned approach to access control.

When it comes to advanced IAM policies, one of the key concepts is policy conditions.

Policy conditions allow you to define circumstances under which a policy should or should not be applied.

For example, you can create a policy condition that grants access only during specific time windows or restricts access to certain IP ranges.

This level of control helps you align access permissions with your organization's security and compliance requirements.

Another advanced IAM policy feature is the use of policy variables.

Policy variables enable dynamic access control by allowing you to refer to attributes of the request, such as the requester's IP address or the current date.

By using variables, you can create policies that adapt to changing conditions, ensuring that access is granted or denied based on real-time information.

Moreover, advanced IAM policies offer the capability to define resource-level permissions.

Rather than granting broad access to an entire service or resource type, you can specify permissions at a granular level.

For instance, you can allow a user to read but not modify specific records in a database, providing a higher degree of control over data access.

Role assignments are the means by which IAM policies are attached to individuals, groups, or services within your cloud environment.

Advanced role assignments go beyond the basic "read" or "write" permissions.

They involve the precise mapping of permissions to roles based on the principle of least privilege.

A role assignment might be designed to grant a developer access to a specific S3 bucket for a limited duration, or it could provide an auditor with read-only access to a subset of resources.

Additionally, advanced IAM policies and role assignments can incorporate the use of external identity providers (IdPs).

Federated identity is a mechanism by which external IdPs, such as Active Directory or an SSO provider, can be integrated with your cloud environment.

This enables users to sign in using their existing corporate credentials, simplifying user management and enhancing security.

Conditional role assignments can also be tied to federated identities, allowing for even greater flexibility in access control.

For example, you can grant temporary elevated permissions to users when they sign in from specific locations or during particular times.

When managing advanced IAM policies and role assignments, it's crucial to adopt a structured approach.

Consider using naming conventions for policies and roles that provide clarity and help you keep track of their purpose. Organize policies into logical groups or hierarchies to simplify administration and prevent policy sprawl.

Additionally, implement versioning and change management practices to track and review modifications to policies and role assignments.

Advanced IAM also extends to the use of custom policies and policy documents.

While cloud providers offer predefined policies, custom policies allow you to craft access control rules tailored to your unique requirements.

These custom policies can be highly specific, defining access down to individual resources and actions.

However, with great power comes the need for careful scrutiny and testing to ensure that custom policies do not inadvertently expose vulnerabilities.

In terms of best practices, advanced IAM policies and role assignments should adhere to the principle of least privilege.

This means granting only the minimum permissions necessary to perform a specific task or role.

Avoid granting broad permissions to users or roles, as it increases the potential for misuse or accidental exposure of resources.

Regularly review and audit policies and role assignments to ensure they remain aligned with your organization's security posture.

Maintain a process for periodically validating permissions to identify and rectify any over-privileged or misconfigured access.

Continuous monitoring is an essential part of managing advanced IAM.

Leverage cloud-native or third-party monitoring and alerting solutions to detect and respond to suspicious or unauthorized activities.

These solutions can provide real-time visibility into access patterns, allowing you to identify anomalies and take immediate action.

Advanced IAM policies can also integrate with other security mechanisms, such as Identity and Access Management (IAM) roles.

These roles enable you to grant temporary permissions to services or resources, such as EC2 instances or Lambda functions, without needing long-term credentials.

By attaching an IAM role to a resource, you can ensure that it only has the necessary permissions for its specific tasks, reducing the attack surface.

Furthermore, consider implementing multi-factor authentication (MFA) for users and roles with elevated privileges.

MFA adds an additional layer of security by requiring users to provide multiple forms of verification before gaining access.

By implementing MFA for administrative roles or sensitive operations, you can significantly enhance your security posture.

In summary, advanced IAM policies and role assignments are fundamental components of a robust cloud security strategy.

They provide the means to finely control access to cloud resources, incorporate external identity providers, and implement conditional access policies.

Best practices include following the principle of least privilege, structuring policies logically, and regularly auditing and monitoring access.

By leveraging advanced IAM features, you can strengthen your cloud security and align it with your organization's unique requirements and compliance standards.

Automated user provisioning and deprovisioning play a vital role in ensuring the security and efficiency of an organization's digital identity management.

In the modern workplace, where employees frequently join and leave organizations, the process of managing user accounts can be challenging and time-consuming.

Automated user provisioning addresses this challenge by streamlining the creation, modification, and removal of user accounts across various systems and applications.

When a new employee joins an organization, automated provisioning enables IT teams to quickly set up the necessary accounts and access rights, ensuring that the employee has the resources needed to perform their job.

This process often involves the integration of identity and access management (IAM) solutions that connect HR systems, directories, and applications, allowing for seamless account creation.

Furthermore, automated provisioning helps maintain consistency in user access across the organization, reducing the likelihood of errors or security gaps resulting from manual processes.

It ensures that user access rights are granted based on predefined roles and permissions, which can be aligned with an organization's security policies.

For example, a new employee may be automatically assigned the role of a "marketing manager" with corresponding access to marketing-related applications and data.

Automated provisioning can also enforce password policies and multifactor authentication (MFA) requirements during the user onboarding process, enhancing security from the outset.

In addition to user provisioning, automated deprovisioning is equally important.

When an employee leaves an organization or changes roles, deprovisioning ensures that their access to systems and applications is promptly revoked.

This is crucial for security reasons, as former employees with lingering access pose a significant risk to an organization's data and resources.

Automated deprovisioning helps mitigate these risks by immediately revoking access rights, reducing the window of vulnerability.

It also simplifies the offboarding process, enabling IT teams to efficiently remove user accounts and associated access.

A key benefit of automated deprovisioning is its ability to perform bulk updates or removals when multiple users experience status changes simultaneously.

For instance, if a department undergoes a reorganization, automated deprovisioning can swiftly adjust access rights for affected employees.

Furthermore, automated user deprovisioning can help organizations maintain compliance with regulatory requirements.

For instance, regulations like the General Data Protection Regulation (GDPR) require organizations to ensure that user data is not retained longer than necessary.

Automated deprovisioning can assist in this regard by automatically deleting or archiving user accounts and data once they are no longer needed.

To effectively implement automated user provisioning and deprovisioning, organizations should follow a structured approach.

This includes defining clear user roles and permissions, establishing workflows for provisioning and deprovisioning, and integrating IAM solutions with HR systems and application directories.

Organizations should also regularly review and update access policies and workflows to reflect changes in their environment and personnel.

It's essential to have a process in place for auditing and monitoring user provisioning and deprovisioning activities.

Regularly reviewing logs and access reports can help identify anomalies or unauthorized changes, allowing organizations to take prompt action.

When selecting IAM solutions for automated provisioning and deprovisioning, organizations should consider factors such as scalability, compatibility with existing systems, and the ability to support various authentication methods.

Furthermore, organizations should prioritize security measures, such as role-based access control and MFA, to enhance the overall security posture.

As with any automated process, there are potential challenges to consider.

One challenge is ensuring that automated provisioning and deprovisioning systems are correctly configured and synchronized with all relevant systems and applications.

Failure to do so can result in discrepancies in user access, leading to security risks.

Additionally, organizations should be mindful of the potential for "orphaned" accounts, where user access remains active even after an employee has left the organization.

Proactive monitoring and regular audits can help address this issue.

Another challenge is managing exceptions.

While automated provisioning and deprovisioning can handle standard scenarios efficiently, there may be exceptions that require manual intervention.

For instance, certain access requests or terminations may require approval from supervisors or department heads.

Organizations should establish clear procedures for handling exceptions to ensure that they are addressed promptly.

In summary, automated user provisioning and deprovisioning are critical components of modern identity and access management.

They streamline the process of granting and revoking user access, enhancing security, and operational efficiency.

By implementing robust workflows, integrating systems, and following best practices, organizations can ensure that their automated provisioning and deprovisioning processes are effective and secure.

Chapter 5: Continuous Monitoring and Remediation

Implementing continuous security monitoring is a crucial aspect of maintaining the security posture of an organization's digital assets. It involves the ongoing and systematic surveillance of an organization's IT environment to identify and respond to security threats and vulnerabilities. Continuous security monitoring helps organizations detect and mitigate security incidents in real-time, minimizing potential damage. It is an essential component of a proactive cybersecurity strategy, allowing organizations to stay one step ahead of cyber threats. Continuous security monitoring operates on the principle that cybersecurity is not a one-time effort but an ongoing process that requires constant vigilance. In today's digital landscape, where cyber threats are constantly evolving, traditional periodic security assessments are no longer sufficient. Instead, organizations need to continuously monitor their networks, systems, and applications to identify and respond to threats as they arise. Continuous security monitoring encompasses various activities and technologies designed to protect an organization's assets and data. One of its core components is the collection and analysis of security-related data from multiple sources. This data can include logs, network traffic, system configurations, and information from security sensors and intrusion detection systems. By analyzing this data, organizations can gain insights into their security posture and quickly identify abnormal or suspicious activities. To effectively implement continuous security monitoring, organizations should establish a clear strategy and framework. This includes defining what needs to be monitored, how data will be collected, and which tools and technologies will be used. A crucial aspect of this strategy is the establishment of security baselines, which represent the normal state of an organization's IT environment. Baselines help organizations identify deviations from the norm, which could indicate a security incident. Implementing continuous security monitoring also involves setting up automated alerting mechanisms. These alerts can notify security teams when specific thresholds or anomalies are detected, allowing for swift responses to potential threats. Automation plays a significant role in continuous security monitoring because it can reduce the burden on security personnel. For example, automated scripts can perform routine security checks and assessments, freeing up human analysts to focus on more complex tasks. Additionally, automation can help organizations respond to security incidents faster, minimizing the impact of potential breaches. Continuous security monitoring tools and technologies come in various forms. Security information and event management (SIEM) systems are one of the most commonly used tools. SIEM solutions collect and analyze log data from various sources to identify security events. They correlate data to create a comprehensive view of an organization's security landscape. Intrusion detection systems (IDS) and intrusion prevention systems (IPS) are also essential components of continuous security monitoring. IDS solutions detect suspicious activities or patterns in network traffic, while IPS solutions can take automated actions to block or mitigate threats. Vulnerability scanners are another key tool for continuous security monitoring. These scanners identify vulnerabilities in systems and applications, allowing organizations to prioritize and remediate security weaknesses. Furthermore, endpoint detection and response (EDR) solutions provide continuous monitoring of endpoints, such as computers and mobile devices. EDR solutions can detect and respond to threats at the endpoint level, providing an additional layer of security.

Cloud security posture management (CSPM) tools help organizations monitor and assess their cloud infrastructure's security. These tools can identify misconfigurations and compliance issues within cloud environments, ensuring that organizations maintain robust security in the cloud. Implementing continuous security monitoring also involves defining incident response procedures. When a security incident is detected, organizations must have clear guidelines for how to respond. This includes defining roles and responsibilities, communication plans, and escalation procedures. Regularly testing and updating incident response plans is crucial to ensuring an effective response to security incidents. Continuous security monitoring is not limited to on-premises environments. With the increasing adoption of cloud services and remote work, organizations need to extend their monitoring capabilities to the cloud and remote endpoints. Cloud-native security solutions and remote monitoring tools are essential for addressing these challenges. Another vital aspect of continuous security monitoring is threat intelligence. Organizations should stay informed about the latest cybersecurity threats and vulnerabilities. Threat intelligence feeds can provide valuable information about emerging threats, helping organizations adapt their monitoring strategies accordingly. While continuous security monitoring is essential, it does come with challenges. One challenge is the sheer volume of data generated by monitoring tools. Organizations may struggle to sift through and analyze this data effectively. To address this challenge, machine learning and artificial intelligence (AI) technologies can be employed to automate the analysis of large datasets and identify patterns indicative of security threats. Another challenge is the need for skilled security personnel to manage and respond to alerts generated by monitoring systems. The cybersecurity skills gap can make it difficult for organizations to find and retain qualified security professionals. To overcome this challenge, organizations may consider outsourcing some or all of their continuous security monitoring to managed security service providers (MSSPs). MSSPs can offer expertise and round-the-clock monitoring services, reducing the burden on in-house teams. In summary, implementing continuous security monitoring is a fundamental aspect of modern cybersecurity. It involves the ongoing surveillance of an organization's IT environment to detect and respond to security threats and vulnerabilities. Continuous security monitoring requires a well-defined strategy, automated alerting mechanisms, and the use of various tools and technologies, including SIEM systems, IDS/IPS solutions, vulnerability scanners, EDR, CSPM tools, and threat intelligence. While challenges exist, organizations that prioritize continuous security monitoring can better protect their digital assets and data from evolving cyber threats. In today's dynamic and ever-evolving cybersecurity landscape, organizations face a constant barrage of security threats and vulnerabilities that can put their digital assets and data at risk. As a result, it has become essential for businesses to implement automated remediation strategies to swiftly address security issues and minimize potential damage. Automated remediation is the process of using technology and predefined actions to automatically respond to and mitigate security incidents, vulnerabilities, or compliance violations. These automated responses can help organizations reduce the time it takes to identify and remediate security issues, improving their overall security posture. Automated remediation is a critical component of a proactive and effective cybersecurity strategy. It enables organizations to not only detect security incidents but also respond to them in real-time or near-real-time, reducing the window of opportunity for attackers. By automating the remediation of security issues, organizations can achieve several key benefits, including increased efficiency, reduced human error, and enhanced security resilience. One of the primary advantages of automated remediation is its ability to significantly improve incident response times. When a security incident occurs, automated systems can instantly trigger predefined actions, such as isolating compromised systems, blocking malicious IP addresses, or applying security patches. This rapid response can help contain the incident, prevent further damage, and limit the exposure of sensitive data. Automation also plays a vital role in reducing human error. Security teams often face the challenge of handling a large volume of alerts and incidents, which can lead to fatigue and oversights. Automated remediation can handle routine, repetitive tasks consistently and accurately, eliminating the risk of human error. Additionally, automation can assist organizations in maintaining a consistent security posture by ensuring that security policies and configurations are continuously enforced. By automatically applying security patches, updates, and configuration changes, organizations can reduce the likelihood of security gaps resulting from overlooked tasks. Automated remediation can be applied to a wide range of security issues, including malware infections, phishing attacks, unauthorized access attempts, and compliance violations. For instance, when a security system detects a malware infection on an endpoint, automated remediation can isolate the affected device from the network, initiate a scan and removal process, and notify the security team. Similarly, in the case of a phishing attack, automated remediation can block the malicious email sender, delete the phishing email from user inboxes, and reset compromised passwords. Automated remediation can also address vulnerabilities identified through vulnerability scanning and assessment tools. When a critical vulnerability is detected, automated systems can automatically apply security patches or configuration changes to remediate the issue. This proactive approach helps organizations stay ahead of potential exploits and minimize their exposure to cyber threats. To implement effective automated remediation, organizations must first define their remediation policies and procedures. These policies should outline the specific actions to be taken in response to different types of security incidents, vulnerabilities, or compliance violations. For example, the policy may specify that malware-infected devices should be isolated from the network, while unpatched systems should receive automated updates. Once the policies are defined, organizations can configure their security systems, such as intrusion detection systems (IDS), intrusion prevention systems (IPS), endpoint security solutions, and vulnerability management platforms, to execute automated remediation actions based on predefined triggers and conditions. Automation orchestration platforms and security information and event management (SIEM) systems play a crucial role in coordinating and managing automated remediation efforts. These platforms can centralize security data, correlate information from various sources, and trigger automated responses based on predefined playbooks or workflows. Security teams can customize these playbooks to suit their organization's specific needs and risk tolerance. Furthermore, automated remediation can be integrated with threat intelligence feeds to enhance its effectiveness. By leveraging threat intelligence data, organizations can proactively identify emerging threats and automate responses to block or mitigate these threats before they can exploit vulnerabilities. Automated remediation can also extend into the cloud, where organizations can leverage cloud-native security tools and services to enforce security policies and remediate issues in cloud environments. For example, cloud security posture management (CSPM) tools can continuously monitor cloud configurations and automatically remediate misconfigurations or non-compliance with security policies. While automated remediation offers numerous benefits, it is not without challenges and considerations. Organizations must strike a balance between automation and human oversight to ensure that automated responses do not inadvertently disrupt business operations or introduce new risks. There is also the risk of false positives, where automated systems mistakenly trigger responses to non-threatening events. To mitigate these risks, organizations should implement robust testing, validation, and monitoring processes to ensure that automated remediation actions align with their security objectives. Additionally, organizations must remain vigilant about keeping their automation scripts, policies, and playbooks up-to-date to address evolving threats and vulnerabilities. Furthermore, automation should complement human decision-making rather than replace it entirely. Human analysts still play a crucial role in understanding the context of security incidents, conducting root cause analysis, and making informed decisions about appropriate remediation actions. In summary, automated remediation strategies are essential in today's cybersecurity landscape. They enable organizations to respond rapidly to security incidents, vulnerabilities, and compliance violations while reducing the risk of human error and maintaining a consistent security posture. By defining clear policies, leveraging automation orchestration platforms, and integrating threat intelligence, organizations can optimize their automated remediation efforts and enhance their overall security resilience.

Chapter 6: Compliance as Code in the Cloud

Implementing compliance checks as code is a critical practice in modern cybersecurity and compliance management. It involves integrating compliance checks and validations into the software development and deployment pipelines. By doing so, organizations can ensure that compliance is continuously monitored and enforced throughout the software development lifecycle. This approach aligns with the concept of "compliance as code" or "policy as code," which involves codifying compliance requirements and automating their evaluation. One of the key benefits of implementing compliance checks as code is the ability to identify and address compliance issues early in the development process. Traditionally, compliance checks were conducted manually or as part of separate auditing processes after software was deployed. This often led to delays in identifying and remediating compliance violations, increasing the risk of non-compliance. With compliance checks as code, organizations can catch compliance issues at the earliest stages of development, allowing developers to fix them before they become more costly to address. Another advantage of this approach is consistency. Compliance checks as code ensures that compliance requirements are applied consistently across all software components and environments, reducing the risk of configuration drift or human error. Additionally, it promotes transparency by providing a clear and automated record of compliance checks, making it easier to demonstrate compliance to auditors and stakeholders. Implementing compliance checks as code requires several key steps and considerations. First, organizations need to define their compliance requirements and translate them into machine-readable formats. This typically involves creating compliance policies, standards, or templates that can be expressed as code. For example, compliance requirements related to data encryption, access controls, or configuration settings can be defined in code using a domain-specific language or declarative syntax. Once compliance requirements are codified, organizations need to integrate them into their software development and deployment pipelines. This may involve using infrastructure as code (IaC) tools, configuration management systems, or continuous integration/continuous deployment (CI/CD) pipelines to automate compliance checks. For example, IaC templates can be augmented with compliance rules that specify how resources should be provisioned and configured to meet compliance requirements. During the build and deployment process, these templates are evaluated, and any non-compliant configurations are flagged for remediation. Organizations also need to consider the tools and technologies they will use to implement compliance checks as code. There are various tools and frameworks available for this purpose, including open-source solutions and commercial products. These tools can help automate compliance scanning, evaluate configurations against predefined policies, and generate reports on compliance status. Choosing the right tooling depends on an organization's specific compliance needs, technology stack, and budget. Furthermore, organizations should establish processes for managing and maintaining compliance checks as code. As software evolves and compliance requirements change, it's essential to update and version control compliance policies and rules. This ensures that the compliance checks remain relevant and effective over time. Additionally, organizations should establish workflows for handling compliance violations when they are detected. Automated remediation actions can be defined to address common compliance issues, while more complex or critical violations may require manual intervention. A critical aspect of implementing compliance checks as code is testing. Organizations should thoroughly test their compliance checks to ensure they accurately evaluate configurations and identify non-compliance. This includes both unit testing of individual compliance rules and end-to-end testing of the entire compliance checking process within the CI/CD pipeline. Test automation can help identify and address issues early in the development process. Finally, organizations should consider the cultural aspects of implementing compliance checks as code. This approach often involves a cultural shift, as developers, operations teams, and compliance experts need to collaborate closely to define, implement, and maintain compliance checks. Clear communication and collaboration are key to successfully integrating compliance into the development process. In summary, implementing compliance checks as code is a proactive and effective approach to ensuring continuous compliance in software development and deployment. By codifying compliance requirements, automating compliance checks, and integrating them into development pipelines, organizations can identify and address compliance issues early, maintain consistency, and demonstrate compliance to auditors and stakeholders. However, it requires careful planning, well-defined processes, appropriate tooling, and a cultural shift toward collaboration and automation to be successful in the long run.

Automated compliance scanning and reporting have become indispensable components of modern cybersecurity and regulatory compliance efforts. These practices involve leveraging technology to automatically assess an organization's adherence to various compliance standards and regulations. By doing so, organizations can efficiently identify and rectify non-compliance issues while minimizing manual effort and the risk of human error. One of the primary benefits of automated compliance scanning is its ability to provide continuous monitoring and real-time feedback. Traditional compliance assessments were typically conducted periodically, which left organizations exposed to compliance gaps between assessments. In contrast, automated scanning can evaluate an organization's compliance posture continuously, allowing it to detect and address non-compliance promptly. This real-time visibility into compliance status is invaluable for organizations operating in dynamic and rapidly changing environments. Automated compliance scanning also improves efficiency and reduces the burden on compliance teams. Manually assessing compliance across an organization's IT infrastructure can be a time-consuming and resource-intensive process. However, automation streamlines this process by leveraging software tools to perform assessments quickly and accurately. This frees up compliance professionals to focus on higher-value tasks, such as analyzing results, implementing corrective actions, and ensuring that compliance efforts align with the organization's strategic goals. Moreover, automation can help organizations scale their compliance efforts as their IT environments grow or evolve. As new systems, applications, and services are deployed, automated scanning can be extended to cover these additions, ensuring that compliance is maintained across the entire infrastructure. Automated compliance scanning relies on the use of specialized software tools and platforms designed to evaluate an organization's systems, configurations, and data against predefined compliance standards and regulations. These tools employ a combination of predefined rules, policies, and checks to assess various aspects of an organization's IT environment, such as security settings, access controls, data protection measures, and more. Common compliance standards that can be automated include the Payment Card Industry Data Security Standard (PCI DSS), the Health Insurance Portability and Accountability Act (HIPAA), the General Data Protection Regulation (GDPR), and many others. Automated compliance scanning tools are typically configured to scan and assess a wide range of IT assets, including servers, workstations, network devices, databases, and cloud resources. Once scanning is complete, these tools generate detailed reports that highlight compliance violations, vulnerabilities, and areas of concern. These reports are invaluable for organizations seeking to maintain and demonstrate their compliance posture. Automated compliance scanning is not a one-size-fits-all solution, as different organizations have unique compliance needs and IT environments. As a result, organizations must carefully select and configure the scanning tools that best meet their specific requirements. Factors to consider when choosing an automated compliance scanning tool include the comprehensiveness of compliance checks, integration capabilities with existing systems, scalability, ease of use, and the tool's ability to support the organization's compliance objectives. Another important aspect of automated compliance scanning is remediation. Identifying non-compliance issues is just the first step; organizations must also take action to remediate these issues promptly. Some automated scanning tools offer built-in remediation capabilities, allowing them to automatically correct certain compliance violations. For example, a tool may automatically adjust security settings or apply patches to address vulnerabilities. However, not all issues can be remediated automatically, and some may require manual intervention.

In these cases, the scanning tool should provide guidance and documentation to help compliance teams resolve the issues effectively. It's essential to emphasize the role of reporting in automated compliance scanning. Compliance reports generated by scanning tools serve multiple purposes. They provide an overview of an organization's compliance status, identify areas that require attention, and offer insights into potential risks. Moreover, these reports are instrumental when interacting with auditors, regulators, or other stakeholders. They serve as a comprehensive record of an organization's compliance efforts, demonstrating its commitment to adhering to relevant standards and regulations. Additionally, compliance reports can help organizations make data-driven decisions about where to allocate resources for remediation and improvement. Implementing automated compliance scanning is not a one-time endeavor but an ongoing process. Compliance standards and regulations evolve, as do an organization's IT infrastructure and practices. As such, organizations must regularly update and fine-tune their automated scanning processes to remain effective and aligned with compliance requirements. This involves revisiting compliance policies, rules, and checks to ensure they reflect the latest standards and best practices. It also includes adjusting scanning configurations to accommodate changes in the IT environment and compliance objectives. Furthermore, organizations must establish clear processes for responding to the findings of automated scans. This includes defining roles and responsibilities for remediation, setting priorities for addressing non-compliance issues, and establishing workflows for tracking and documenting corrective actions. In summary, automated compliance scanning and reporting are crucial tools for organizations striving to meet regulatory requirements and maintain strong cybersecurity postures. By automating the assessment of compliance with predefined standards and regulations, organizations can achieve continuous monitoring, efficiency, and scalability. Selecting the right scanning tools, ensuring they align with an organization's unique compliance needs, and establishing robust remediation and reporting processes are key steps in implementing an effective automated compliance scanning program. Remember that compliance is an ongoing effort, and organizations must regularly update and refine their automated scanning processes to adapt to changing compliance requirements and IT landscapes.

Chapter 7: Cloud Security Orchestration and Automation

Orchestration workflow design for security is a fundamental aspect of modern cybersecurity strategies. It involves the careful planning, creation, and execution of automated workflows that enhance an organization's security posture. These workflows are designed to streamline security processes, improve incident response, and reduce the risk of security breaches. One of the key goals of orchestration workflow design is to enable security teams to respond to security events quickly and effectively. In today's complex threat landscape, where cyberattacks can occur at any moment, automation plays a crucial role in minimizing response times. Security orchestration workflows can be designed to handle a wide range of security tasks, from threat detection and alerting to incident investigation and mitigation. The design process begins with a thorough understanding of an organization's security requirements, its existing security tools and technologies, and its incident response procedures. With this knowledge, security professionals can start to identify opportunities for automation and orchestration. The next step is to define the specific workflows that will be created. These workflows should align with the organization's security policies and address its most critical security needs. For example, a common use case for orchestration workflow design is automating the response to security alerts generated by intrusion detection systems (IDS) and security information and event management (SIEM) platforms. In this scenario, a workflow might involve the automatic isolation of compromised systems, the collection of forensic data, and the notification of relevant personnel. The design phase also includes specifying the triggers that will initiate the workflows. Triggers can be events such as the detection of a suspicious file or an unauthorized login attempt. Once the workflows and triggers are defined, the next step is to select the appropriate orchestration tools and technologies. These tools are responsible for executing the workflows and coordinating the actions of various security systems and components. Common security orchestration platforms include Security Orchestration, Automation, and Response (SOAR) solutions and workflow automation tools. The chosen tools should be capable of integrating with existing security infrastructure, including firewalls, antivirus solutions, and incident response systems. They should also support the creation of custom connectors or integrations to bridge gaps between different security technologies. As the design process progresses, it's essential to consider the scalability of the orchestration workflows. Organizations should anticipate changes in their IT environments, such as the addition of new assets or services, and ensure that their workflows can adapt accordingly. Flexibility is a key characteristic of effective security orchestration. Additionally, organizations should regularly review and update their workflows to account for changes in threat landscapes and emerging attack techniques. Another critical aspect of orchestration workflow design is ensuring that the workflows are well-documented. Comprehensive documentation includes detailed descriptions of each workflow, their associated triggers, and the expected outcomes. Documentation should also outline the roles and responsibilities of personnel involved in the execution and oversight of the workflows. This documentation serves as a valuable resource for training security teams and for auditing and compliance purposes. The design of security orchestration workflows should also incorporate considerations for security and access control. Access to the orchestration system and the workflows themselves should be restricted to authorized personnel only. This helps prevent misuse or unauthorized access to critical security processes. Moreover, encryption and secure communication protocols should be employed to protect the integrity and confidentiality of data transmitted within the workflows. Testing and validation are crucial steps in the design process. Before deploying orchestration workflows in a production environment, they should undergo thorough testing to ensure that they function as intended. Testing involves simulating various security scenarios and verifying that the workflows can respond appropriately. Additionally, testing helps identify any potential bottlenecks or issues that could affect the performance of the orchestration system. Once the workflows are deployed, ongoing monitoring and maintenance are essential. Security teams should continuously monitor the execution of workflows to detect any anomalies or errors. Regular maintenance includes updating workflows to incorporate new threat intelligence, patches, or security best practices. Organizations should also conduct periodic reviews to assess the effectiveness of their security orchestration workflows. This evaluation process can help identify areas for improvement and optimization. Furthermore, feedback from security analysts who use the workflows in real-world situations can provide valuable insights for refinement. In summary, orchestration workflow design for security is a critical component of modern cybersecurity strategies. Effective design involves understanding an organization's security needs, defining workflows, selecting appropriate tools, and ensuring scalability and flexibility. Documentation, security controls, testing, and ongoing monitoring are integral parts of the design and deployment process. By carefully designing and implementing security orchestration workflows, organizations can enhance their ability to respond to security incidents rapidly and efficiently, ultimately strengthening their overall security posture. Security incident response automation is a vital aspect of modern cybersecurity strategies, streamlining the handling of security incidents to mitigate potential damage. It involves automating various aspects of the incident response process to detect, investigate, and remediate security threats more efficiently. Automating incident response can significantly reduce response times, minimize the risk of human error, and help organizations maintain a robust security posture. One of the key objectives of security incident response automation is to accelerate the detection of security incidents. In a rapidly evolving threat landscape, early detection is crucial for preventing or minimizing the impact of security breaches. Automation can enable organizations to monitor their IT environments continuously, looking for signs of suspicious or malicious activities. For example, automated monitoring tools can analyze network traffic, system logs, and user behavior patterns to identify anomalies that may indicate a security incident. Additionally, automation can help organizations create predefined alerting rules that trigger notifications when specific conditions are met, allowing security teams to respond proactively. Another essential aspect of security incident response automation is the ability to investigate incidents more effectively. When a potential security incident is detected, automation can assist in collecting relevant data and evidence quickly. This might include capturing network packet captures, system logs, and memory snapshots. Automation can also help security analysts perform initial triage, categorizing incidents based on their severity and providing contextual information. Furthermore, automation can support incident correlation by aggregating information from various security tools and data sources, allowing analysts to gain a more comprehensive view of an incident. Automated incident investigation workflows can also aid in determining the scope of an incident, identifying affected systems and assets. Remediation is a critical component of incident response, and automation can greatly assist in this phase. Automated response actions can be predefined and executed when specific types of incidents occur. For instance, when a malware infection is detected on an endpoint, automated remediation may involve isolating the infected device from the network, blocking malicious communication, and initiating the removal of malware. Automation can also help with containment strategies, such as quarantining compromised user accounts or systems. Furthermore, it can assist in incident remediation by facilitating the deployment of patches or updates to vulnerable systems. A significant advantage of security incident response automation is its ability to improve consistency and reduce the likelihood of human error. Human responders may inadvertently skip steps or make mistakes during the incident response process, which can lead to incomplete or ineffective responses. Automation ensures that predefined response actions are executed consistently and accurately. This consistency is essential for maintaining a high level of security across an organization's IT infrastructure. Moreover, automation can help organizations manage incident response at scale. In large enterprises or cloud environments, numerous security incidents may occur simultaneously or in quick succession. Automation can handle multiple incidents simultaneously, allowing security teams to address a higher volume of incidents without sacrificing response quality. To implement security incident response automation effectively, organizations should start by defining clear incident response workflows. These workflows outline the specific steps to be taken when different types of incidents occur. The workflows should be developed collaboratively with input from various stakeholders, including security analysts, IT administrators, and legal and compliance teams. Once the workflows are defined, organizations can select and configure automation tools and technologies. These tools should support integration with existing security systems, data sources, and communication channels. For example, automation tools should be able to connect with intrusion detection systems (IDS), security information and event management (SIEM) platforms, and incident ticketing systems. Custom integrations or connectors may be required to bridge any gaps between different technologies. It's essential to ensure that automation solutions align with an organization's security policies and regulatory requirements. Security teams should also consider access controls and permissions, restricting access to automation systems and workflows to authorized personnel only. Encryption and secure communication should be implemented to protect sensitive data and ensure that automation commands and responses are secure. Testing and validation are crucial aspects of implementing security incident response automation. Before deploying automation in a production environment, organizations should thoroughly test the workflows, response actions, and integrations. Testing should simulate various security scenarios to ensure that the automation system responds effectively to different types of incidents. Additionally, organizations should conduct tabletop exercises and drills to train security teams on how to use automation tools and workflows during real incidents. Maintenance and continuous improvement are essential for the long-term success of security incident response automation. Organizations should regularly review and update their workflows and response actions to align with changes in the threat landscape and evolving attack techniques. Incident response automation should be part of a broader incident response plan, which is regularly reviewed and tested. Feedback from security analysts and incident responders who use the automation tools in real-world scenarios can provide valuable insights for optimization. In summary, security incident response automation is a critical component of modern cybersecurity strategies. It enhances an organization's ability to detect, investigate, and remediate security incidents promptly and efficiently. By automating various aspects of incident response, organizations can reduce response times, improve consistency, and effectively manage incidents at scale. However, successful implementation requires careful planning, testing, and ongoing maintenance to ensure that automation aligns with security policies and regulatory requirements and continues to meet the organization's evolving needs.

Chapter 8: Advanced Threat Detection and Response

Advanced threat detection techniques are a critical component of modern cybersecurity strategies, designed to identify and mitigate sophisticated and evolving threats that may evade traditional security measures. These techniques leverage advanced technologies and methodologies to enhance an organization's ability to detect and respond to cyber threats effectively. One of the key principles behind advanced threat detection is the recognition that traditional security solutions, while essential, may not be sufficient to protect against the full spectrum of cyber threats. Attackers continually develop new tactics, techniques, and procedures (TTPs) to bypass or evade traditional security controls. As a result, organizations need to adopt a proactive approach to identify and neutralize these threats before they can cause harm.

Machine learning and artificial intelligence (AI) play a pivotal role in advanced threat detection techniques. These technologies enable security solutions to analyze vast amounts of data quickly and identify patterns that may indicate a security threat. Machine learning algorithms can process data from various sources, including network traffic, system logs, and user behavior, to detect anomalies and deviations from normal patterns. By continuously learning and adapting, machine learning models become more effective at identifying new and previously unknown threats.

Behavioral analytics is another advanced threat detection technique that focuses on understanding and monitoring user and entity behavior. This approach establishes a baseline of normal behavior for users and devices within an organization. Any deviations from this baseline, such as unusual access patterns, unexpected data transfers, or abnormal system activity, can trigger alerts for further investigation. Behavioral analytics can help organizations detect insider threats and external attackers who have gained unauthorized access to systems.

Threat intelligence feeds and feeds from open-source intelligence (OSINT) provide organizations with valuable information about the latest threats and attack techniques. Advanced threat detection solutions can ingest and analyze threat intelligence data to identify indicators of compromise (IoCs) and signatures associated with known threats. This proactive approach allows organizations to identify and respond to threats more rapidly.

Sandboxing is a technique that involves executing potentially malicious code or files in an isolated environment, known as a sandbox, to observe their behavior without risking harm to the production network. Sandboxing helps identify zero-day exploits and malware that may have evaded traditional signature-based detection methods. By observing how the code behaves in the sandbox, security teams can determine if it exhibits malicious behavior.

Endpoint detection and response (EDR) solutions are essential components of advanced threat detection techniques. These solutions focus on monitoring and responding to security events at the endpoint, which may include workstations, servers, and mobile devices. EDR solutions provide real-time visibility into endpoint activities and can detect suspicious processes, file changes, and registry modifications. They also offer the capability to respond to threats by isolating compromised endpoints or containing malicious processes.

Network traffic analysis is crucial for identifying advanced threats that may traverse an organization's network. Advanced threat detection solutions can analyze network traffic for unusual or suspicious patterns, such as command-

and-control traffic, lateral movement, and data exfiltration attempts. By correlating network traffic data with other sources of information, such as threat intelligence and endpoint logs, security teams can gain a more comprehensive view of potential threats.

Advanced threat detection techniques also encompass the use of deception technologies. Deception solutions create decoy assets, such as fake servers, endpoints, or data, to lure attackers into revealing themselves. When an attacker interacts with a decoy asset, the deception solution generates alerts, providing early warning of an intrusion. Deception technologies can help organizations detect and respond to threats before they can move laterally within the network.

Advanced threat detection techniques are not limited to identifying threats at the network or endpoint level. They also extend to the cloud and application layer. Cloud security posture management (CSPM) solutions can assess cloud infrastructure configurations for security vulnerabilities and misconfigurations. Application security testing, including static application security testing (SAST) and dynamic application security testing (DAST), can identify vulnerabilities within software applications that attackers may exploit.

Continuous monitoring and threat hunting are integral components of advanced threat detection strategies. Threat hunting involves proactively searching for signs of compromise within an organization's environment. Security analysts actively seek out anomalies and indicators of suspicious activity, even if traditional security controls have not raised alarms. Continuous monitoring and threat hunting are essential for identifying advanced threats that may not trigger automated alerts.

Response automation and orchestration play a vital role in advanced threat detection techniques. When a security event is detected, automation can be used to initiate predefined response actions quickly. These actions may include isolating affected systems, blocking malicious IP addresses, and notifying security teams. Orchestrating incident response workflows ensures that response actions are coordinated and executed efficiently.

Threat intelligence sharing and collaboration with external organizations and industry peers are essential for staying ahead of advanced threats. Many organizations participate in information-sharing initiatives and share threat intelligence to benefit from collective knowledge and insights. Sharing threat data can help organizations identify emerging threats and prepare more effectively.

While advanced threat detection techniques offer significant advantages, they also pose challenges. Organizations need to invest in skilled personnel who can operate and maintain advanced threat detection solutions effectively. Additionally, false positives can be a concern, as advanced techniques may trigger alerts for legitimate activities that resemble malicious behavior.

In summary, advanced threat detection techniques are essential for modern cybersecurity strategies. These techniques leverage technologies such as machine learning, behavioral analytics, and sandboxing to identify and respond to sophisticated and evolving threats. By adopting these techniques and integrating them into their security posture, organizations can enhance their ability to detect and mitigate cyber threats effectively. However, successful implementation requires skilled personnel, ongoing monitoring, and collaboration with threat intelligence sharing communities.

In today's rapidly evolving cybersecurity landscape, the integration of threat intelligence is a crucial component of an organization's strategy for responding to cyber threats effectively.

Threat intelligence provides valuable insights into the latest cyber threats, attack techniques, and vulnerabilities that can help organizations proactively defend against potential attacks.

By integrating threat intelligence into their security operations, organizations can enhance their ability to detect, respond to, and mitigate cyber threats in a more timely and effective manner.

One of the primary goals of threat intelligence integration is to provide security teams with actionable information that can help them make informed decisions about how to respond to potential threats.

Threat intelligence feeds, which can come from a variety of sources, including commercial providers, open-source feeds, and information sharing communities, can provide organizations with real-time data about emerging threats.

These feeds often include indicators of compromise (IoCs), such as malicious IP addresses, domain names, and file hashes, which can be used to identify and block malicious activity within an organization's network.

By integrating threat intelligence feeds into their security infrastructure, organizations can automatically correlate incoming network traffic and log data with known IoCs, enabling them to identify and respond to potential threats more quickly.

In addition to IoCs, threat intelligence often includes information about the tactics, techniques, and procedures (TTPs) used by cyber adversaries.

This information can be invaluable for security teams, as it allows them to better understand the behavior of potential attackers and tailor their response strategies accordingly.

For example, if a threat intelligence feed indicates that a particular threat actor group is known for using a specific malware variant, security teams can proactively search for signs of that malware within their network and take steps to mitigate the threat.

Another critical aspect of threat intelligence integration is the automation of response actions. Security teams can create playbooks or workflows that define specific actions to be taken in response to different types of threats.

These playbooks can be triggered automatically when certain conditions are met, such as the detection of a known IoC or the identification of suspicious behavior.

For example, if a threat intelligence feed indicates that a particular IP address is associated with a known botnet, a playbook could be triggered to block all network traffic to and from that IP address.

Automation can significantly reduce response times, allowing organizations to respond to threats more quickly and effectively.

Threat intelligence can also play a crucial role in incident response. When a security incident occurs, having access to relevant threat intelligence can help organizations understand the nature of the attack and the threat actor behind it.

This information can be used to inform incident response efforts, such as determining the appropriate containment and eradication measures and assessing the potential impact of the incident.

In addition to integrating threat intelligence feeds into their security infrastructure, organizations can also benefit from participating in information sharing and collaboration initiatives.

Many industries and sectors have established information sharing communities that allow organizations to share threat intelligence and collaborate on response efforts.

These communities can provide valuable context and insights into emerging threats and trends, as well as opportunities to learn from the experiences of others.

By participating in these communities, organizations can access a broader pool of threat intelligence and benefit from collective knowledge and expertise.

However, it's important to note that effective threat intelligence integration requires careful consideration of the sources and quality of the intelligence being used.

Not all threat intelligence feeds are created equal, and organizations should assess the relevance and reliability of the information they receive.

They should also be mindful of potential false positives and ensure that their security infrastructure can handle the increased volume of data that may result from threat intelligence integration.

Furthermore, organizations should regularly update and validate their threat intelligence sources to ensure that they remain current and accurate.

In summary, threat intelligence integration is a critical component of a modern cybersecurity strategy.

By leveraging threat intelligence feeds and automating response actions, organizations can enhance their ability to detect, respond to, and mitigate cyber threats effectively.

Threat intelligence also plays a vital role in incident response, helping organizations understand the nature of an attack and inform their response efforts.

Participation in information sharing communities further enhances an organization's access to valuable threat intelligence and collective knowledge.

However, organizations should exercise caution in selecting and validating their threat intelligence sources to ensure that they receive accurate and relevant information.

Chapter 9: Cloud Security Metrics and Reporting

In the realm of cloud security, understanding and measuring the effectiveness of your security measures is crucial for safeguarding your digital assets.

Security metrics play a pivotal role in providing insights into the state of your cloud environment's security posture.

One key metric that organizations often track is the number of security incidents or breaches that occur in their cloud infrastructure.

This metric helps organizations understand the frequency and severity of security incidents and can be used to identify trends or patterns that may indicate a need for adjustments in security measures.

Additionally, tracking the time it takes to detect and respond to security incidents is another important metric. A shorter detection and response time can significantly reduce the potential impact of a security breach.

Measuring the number of vulnerabilities or misconfigurations in your cloud environment is also essential. Vulnerabilities can serve as potential entry points for attackers, making it crucial to monitor and address them promptly.

Furthermore, organizations often monitor the rate of successful phishing attacks, which can target both employees and system accounts, posing significant security risks.

The effectiveness of access control measures is another critical metric. Monitoring and evaluating the accuracy and efficiency of access control lists, role-based access control (RBAC), and identity and access management (IAM) policies can help organizations maintain a secure cloud environment.

Cloud environments often consist of multiple accounts, subscriptions, or tenants. Measuring and managing access across these entities is essential to prevent unauthorized access and data breaches.

Another crucial security metric is the rate of successful data breaches, which quantifies the number of incidents where sensitive data is exposed or stolen.

Tracking the number of security patches and updates applied to cloud systems is essential for maintaining a secure environment. Timely patch management can help mitigate known vulnerabilities.

The configuration of security groups and firewalls in a cloud environment is also a vital metric. Any misconfigurations can lead to security vulnerabilities, so organizations must monitor and rectify them promptly.

Additionally, organizations should measure the rate of successful malware infections in their cloud environments. This metric provides insights into the effectiveness of anti-malware solutions.

Monitoring user activity and access patterns is crucial for detecting suspicious behavior and potential insider threats.

The level of encryption used to protect data at rest and in transit is a vital security metric. Strong encryption is essential to safeguard sensitive information.

Another relevant metric is the rate of account lockouts or failed login attempts. Frequent lockouts may indicate unauthorized access attempts.

Security incidents often lead to financial losses. Measuring the financial impact of security incidents can help organizations assess the cost-effectiveness of their security measures.

In addition to incident-related financial losses, organizations may also track the cost of implementing and maintaining security measures, including software, hardware, and personnel.

The number of security assessments or audits conducted in the cloud environment is another valuable metric. Regular assessments can help identify and rectify vulnerabilities.

Cloud providers offer various security services and features. Organizations may measure their utilization of these services to ensure that they are taking full advantage of the available security tools.

The adoption of multi-factor authentication (MFA) can significantly enhance security. Measuring the rate of MFA adoption can help organizations assess their security posture.

Another critical metric is the rate of compliance with industry standards and regulatory requirements. Compliance is often a legal and contractual obligation, and failing to meet these standards can have severe consequences.

Organizations should also track the number of security alerts generated by their cloud security solutions. A high volume of alerts may indicate the need for more efficient threat detection and response processes.

Cloud security incidents can disrupt business operations. Measuring the impact of security incidents on downtime and service availability is crucial for assessing the overall resilience of a cloud environment.

Furthermore, organizations may monitor the level of security awareness and training among employees. Ensuring that employees are well-informed about security best practices is a fundamental aspect of a robust security strategy.

Cloud environments are dynamic, with resources frequently added, modified, or removed. Tracking changes to the cloud environment configuration is essential for identifying potential security risks.

The rate of security assessments and vulnerability scans conducted on cloud assets is another critical metric. Regular assessments can help organizations identify and remediate security weaknesses.

Finally, organizations may measure the rate of security incidents that result from insider threats. Insider threats can be challenging to detect, making this metric important for identifying potential risks.

In summary, security metrics are essential for evaluating and improving the security of cloud environments. These metrics provide valuable insights into the state of security, potential vulnerabilities, and the effectiveness of security measures.

Organizations should carefully select and regularly review these metrics to ensure that their cloud security strategies are robust and aligned with their overall security objectives.

In the ever-evolving landscape of cybersecurity and compliance, automation has emerged as a powerful tool to streamline reporting processes and enhance the security posture of organizations.

Automation, in the context of compliance and security reporting, refers to the use of software, scripts, or tools to collect, analyze, and generate reports on various aspects of an organization's security and compliance.

One of the primary advantages of automated reporting is its ability to save time and reduce human error. Traditional manual reporting can be time-consuming, error-prone, and labor-intensive, often requiring security and compliance professionals to gather and compile data from multiple sources.

With automated reporting, data can be collected from various systems and sources automatically and in real-time. This not only saves time but also ensures that the information is up-to-date and accurate, reducing the risk of reporting errors.

Automated reporting can encompass a wide range of security and compliance areas, including vulnerability management, patch management, access control, identity and access management (IAM), and more.

For example, in the realm of vulnerability management, automated reporting tools can continuously scan an organization's IT infrastructure, identifying vulnerabilities in software, operating systems, and configurations. These tools can then generate reports that provide detailed information on vulnerabilities, their severity, and recommended remediation actions.

Similarly, automated reporting can be applied to patch management, where it can track the status of patches applied to systems and generate reports to ensure that critical patches are not overlooked.

Access control and IAM are also critical areas for automated reporting. Organizations can use automation to monitor user access, permissions, and entitlements, generating reports that highlight any discrepancies or unauthorized access.

Compliance reporting is another essential aspect of automation. Many organizations are subject to various regulatory requirements, such as the General Data Protection Regulation (GDPR), Health Insurance Portability and Accountability Act (HIPAA), or Payment Card Industry Data Security Standard (PCI DSS). These regulations often require organizations to provide regular reports on their compliance efforts.

Automated reporting tools can help organizations collect and analyze the necessary data to demonstrate compliance with these regulations. For example, they can generate reports that show how data is being handled, who has access to it, and what security measures are in place.

Furthermore, automated reporting can assist organizations in demonstrating compliance with internal policies and standards. Companies often have their security policies, procedures, and standards that must be followed. Automated reporting can help ensure that these internal requirements are met and can provide evidence to support internal audits.

One significant advantage of automated reporting is its scalability. As organizations grow and their IT environments become more complex, manual reporting becomes increasingly challenging. Automated tools can scale effortlessly to handle larger and more diverse data sources, making them suitable for organizations of all sizes.

In addition to saving time and reducing errors, automated reporting can also enhance security by providing real-time visibility into an organization's security posture. Security professionals can use automated reports to identify emerging threats, vulnerabilities, and suspicious activities promptly.

Furthermore, automated reporting can help organizations respond quickly to security incidents. When a security event occurs, automated reporting tools can generate incident reports, detailing the nature of the incident, its impact, and the actions taken to mitigate it. This information is crucial for post-incident analysis and remediation.

Automated reporting also promotes transparency and accountability within an organization. By providing clear and comprehensive reports, stakeholders, including executives, auditors, and regulators, can gain insight into an organization's security and compliance efforts. This transparency can build trust and confidence in the organization's ability to protect sensitive data and adhere to regulatory requirements.

However, while automated reporting offers many advantages, it is not without challenges. Implementing automated reporting solutions requires careful planning, configuration, and integration with existing systems. It also necessitates ongoing maintenance to ensure that the reports generated remain accurate and relevant.

Furthermore, organizations must carefully consider the data privacy and security implications of automated reporting. The tools used to collect and process data for reporting must adhere to strict security standards to prevent unauthorized access and data breaches.

Additionally, organizations should regularly review and refine their reporting processes to ensure that they align with their evolving security and compliance needs. As threats and regulations change, reporting requirements may need to be adjusted accordingly.

In summary, automated reporting for compliance and security is a powerful tool that can save time, reduce errors, enhance security, and promote transparency. By automating the collection, analysis, and generation of reports, organizations can gain real-time visibility into their security posture and compliance efforts.

While implementing automated reporting solutions may require initial effort and investment, the long-term benefits in terms of efficiency, accuracy, and security make it a worthwhile endeavor for organizations seeking to stay ahead in the ever-changing landscape of cybersecurity and compliance.

Chapter 10: Best Practices for Secure DevOps in the Cloud

Integrating security into the DevOps pipeline is a crucial practice in modern software development, as it helps organizations build secure applications from the ground up. By seamlessly incorporating security measures into the software development process, organizations can detect and address vulnerabilities at an early stage, reducing the risk of security breaches.

DevOps, short for Development and Operations, is an approach that combines software development and IT operations to streamline the software delivery process. It emphasizes collaboration, automation, and continuous integration and continuous delivery (CI/CD).

Traditionally, security was often seen as an isolated phase that occurred after development, leading to delays and potential security gaps. However, the DevOps movement recognizes the need for security to be integrated into every step of the development and deployment pipeline.

The integration of security into the DevOps pipeline is often referred to as "DevSecOps," which emphasizes the importance of security as an integral part of the DevOps culture.

One of the key principles of integrating security into DevOps is shifting security left in the development process. This means that security considerations are introduced as early as possible in the software development lifecycle, ideally at the planning and design stages.

Security teams collaborate closely with development and operations teams to ensure that security requirements are clearly defined, understood, and implemented throughout the development process.

Static Application Security Testing (SAST) and Dynamic Application Security Testing (DAST) tools are commonly used in DevOps pipelines to scan code and applications for vulnerabilities. These tools help identify and remediate security issues early in the development process.

In addition to automated testing tools, security practitioners can use code analysis and review practices to identify and address security concerns. Code review processes can include security-focused guidelines and checklists to ensure that developers are aware of and follow best practices.

Another essential aspect of integrating security into DevOps is the use of Infrastructure as Code (IaC). With IaC, infrastructure and configuration settings are defined in code, which enables organizations to manage their infrastructure and applications more efficiently.

IaC allows for the automation of security controls, ensuring that security configurations are consistent and can be easily tracked and audited. Security policies and best practices can be codified and enforced as part of the deployment process.

Furthermore, containerization and orchestration technologies, such as Docker and Kubernetes, have become integral to modern software development and can be used to enhance security in DevOps pipelines.

Containers provide a lightweight and consistent environment for applications, making it easier to manage dependencies and isolate applications. Security teams can leverage container security solutions to scan container images for vulnerabilities and ensure that runtime environments are secure.

Kubernetes, as a container orchestration platform, offers features for access control, network segmentation, and resource isolation. Security configurations and policies can be defined and enforced within Kubernetes clusters.

Continuous monitoring and logging are essential components of DevSecOps. Security teams can use monitoring tools and log analysis to detect anomalies and potential security incidents in real-time.

By collecting and analyzing security-related data, organizations can identify and respond to threats quickly. Security information and event management (SIEM) solutions are commonly used to centralize and correlate security data.

Automation is a fundamental principle of DevOps, and it extends to security processes. Security automation involves the use of scripts, workflows, and tools to automate security tasks and responses.

Automated security testing, vulnerability scanning, and incident response play a crucial role in ensuring that security is integrated seamlessly into the DevOps pipeline.

Another aspect of security automation is the use of Continuous Integration and Continuous Delivery (CI/CD) pipelines. CI/CD pipelines automate the build, test, and deployment of code changes, ensuring that applications are continuously updated and delivered to production.

Security checks can be embedded within these pipelines to validate code changes for security compliance. Automated tests can include security-focused tests, such as penetration testing and compliance checks.

One of the challenges in integrating security into DevOps is the cultural shift required within organizations. Security teams need to collaborate closely with development and operations teams, sharing knowledge and responsibilities.

This cultural shift often involves breaking down traditional silos and fostering a shared responsibility for security. It requires education, training, and a commitment to security as a fundamental part of the development process.

Additionally, security teams must keep pace with the rapid development and deployment cycles of DevOps. Security automation and the use of security-focused tools are critical to meeting the demands of DevSecOps.

In summary, integrating security into the DevOps pipeline, known as DevSecOps, is a critical practice for building secure and resilient software applications. It involves shifting security left in the development process, leveraging automation, and fostering a culture of collaboration and shared responsibility.

By implementing security measures at every stage of the software development lifecycle, organizations can proactively identify and address security vulnerabilities, reduce the risk of security breaches, and deliver more secure software to their users. DevSecOps is not just a methodology; it's a mindset that prioritizes security in a fast-paced, agile development world. Automated security testing is a fundamental practice within DevOps processes, ensuring that security vulnerabilities are identified and remediated as early as possible in the software development lifecycle. It is an integral part of the broader DevSecOps approach, which combines development, operations, and security to create a culture of shared responsibility for security. Automated security testing is a proactive measure that helps organizations detect and address security issues before they reach production, reducing the risk of data breaches and other security incidents. In DevOps, the primary goal is to accelerate software development and delivery while maintaining high-quality standards, and automated security testing aligns with this objective. Traditionally, security assessments were performed manually, consuming valuable time and often causing delays in the software release cycle. Automated security testing tools and practices have revolutionized this process by enabling continuous security assessments that keep pace with the rapid development and deployment of software. One of the key benefits of automated security testing is its ability to uncover vulnerabilities in real-time, allowing developers to address them immediately. This shift-left approach ensures that security is considered early in the development process, reducing the cost and effort required to fix issues later in the lifecycle. Automated security testing encompasses various techniques and tools, including static application security testing (SAST), dynamic application security testing (DAST), and interactive application security testing (IAST). SAST tools analyze the source code or binaries of an application to identify vulnerabilities, coding errors, and security flaws. DAST tools, on the other hand, assess a running application to find vulnerabilities from the outside, simulating how an attacker might exploit weaknesses. IAST tools combine aspects of both SAST and DAST, providing a deeper understanding of an application's security posture. In DevOps, these automated testing tools are integrated into the continuous integration and continuous delivery (CI/CD) pipeline. As code changes are committed and builds are triggered, automated security tests run in parallel with other tests to provide rapid feedback to developers. Static analysis tools, such as Checkmarx and Fortify, scan the source code for vulnerabilities and coding errors before code is even compiled. These tools analyze the codebase for known security issues, such as SQL injection, cross-site scripting (XSS), and insecure authentication mechanisms. Static analysis can identify vulnerabilities that may not be apparent through manual code reviews and ensure that coding best practices are followed. Dynamic analysis tools, such as OWASP ZAP and Burp Suite, assess applications while they are running in a test environment. They send HTTP requests and analyze responses to identify security weaknesses, such as exposed APIs, misconfigured security settings, or vulnerabilities that are only visible during runtime. Interactive analysis tools, like Contrast Security and Veracode, combine the strengths of both SAST and DAST by monitoring application behavior and code execution in real-time. They provide detailed insights into an application's security posture while it's being used. One of the key advantages of automated security testing in DevOps is its ability to scale efficiently. Automated tools can scan thousands of lines of code or test multiple applications simultaneously, which would be impractical to achieve manually. This scalability is crucial for organizations that develop and maintain complex software systems with numerous codebases and frequent releases. Moreover, automated security testing provides repeatability and consistency in security assessments. Tests are executed with the same configuration and parameters each time, reducing the likelihood of human error and ensuring consistent results. This reliability is essential in maintaining the security of applications and services. Another significant benefit of automated security testing is the ability to incorporate it into the DevOps workflow seamlessly. Security tests are treated like any other tests in the CI/CD pipeline, enabling developers to receive immediate feedback on code changes. When vulnerabilities are detected, developers can address them promptly and iterate on their code, leading to faster remediation and more secure software. Additionally, automated security testing helps organizations adhere to compliance and regulatory requirements. Many industries have stringent security standards that must be met, such as the Payment Card Industry Data Security Standard (PCI DSS) or the Health Insurance Portability and Accountability Act (HIPAA). Automated security testing can help identify and rectify non-compliant code or configurations, reducing the risk of non-compliance penalties and security breaches. While automated security testing is a powerful tool in DevOps, it's essential to recognize that it's not a silver bullet. It should be part of a broader security strategy that includes other practices like threat modeling, security training, and manual testing. Additionally, automated testing tools are not infallible and may produce false positives or miss certain vulnerabilities. Therefore, human expertise is still required to interpret the results and make informed decisions about prioritizing and addressing security issues. Furthermore, organizations must consider the cost of implementing and maintaining automated security testing tools, as well as the potential impact on development speed. It's crucial to strike a balance between security and agility, ensuring that security measures don't slow down the development process excessively. In summary, automated security testing is a vital component of DevOps processes, helping organizations identify and remediate security vulnerabilities early in the software development lifecycle. By integrating security assessments into the CI/CD pipeline, organizations can ensure that security is considered from the beginning and that security issues are addressed promptly. However, it's essential to use automated security testing in conjunction with other security practices and to balance security with development speed and cost-effectiveness. With the right tools and practices in place, DevOps teams can build and deploy secure software more efficiently and effectively.

Conclusion

In the world of cloud computing, where data and applications traverse virtual landscapes, security and forensics have become paramount. This book bundle, "Cloud Security & Forensics Handbook: Dive Deep into Azure, AWS, and GCP," is a comprehensive guide that takes readers on a journey through the intricate realm of cloud security and forensics within the three major cloud platforms: Azure, AWS, and GCP.

In Book 1, "Cloud Security Essentials: A Beginner's Guide to Azure, AWS, and GCP," we laid the foundation for understanding the fundamental concepts of cloud security. We explored the shared responsibility model, identity and access management, encryption, and the importance of compliance in cloud environments. This book provided newcomers with the knowledge needed to embark on their cloud security journey.

Building on this foundational knowledge, Book 2, "Mastering Cloud Security: Advanced Strategies for Azure, AWS, and GCP," delved deeper into the intricacies of cloud security. We discussed advanced strategies for securing cloud resources, such as network segmentation, microsegmentation, and security as code. Additionally, we explored the integration of security into the DevOps pipeline and the implementation of security automation.

In Book 3, "Cloud Security and Forensics: Investigating Incidents in Azure, AWS, and GCP," we shifted our focus to the critical task of investigating security incidents in the cloud. We explored digital forensics techniques tailored to cloud environments and examined how to collect, analyze, and preserve digital evidence. This book equipped readers with the skills needed to respond effectively to security incidents and breaches.

Finally, in Book 4, "Expert Cloud Security and Compliance Automation: Azure, AWS, and GCP Best Practices," we delved into the world of automation. We discussed security policy implementation as code, compliance scanning, and the orchestration of security workflows. By automating security and compliance processes, organizations can ensure consistency and reduce the risk of human error.

As we conclude this book bundle, it is important to recognize the ever-evolving nature of cloud security and forensics. Azure, AWS, and GCP are continuously evolving, and so are the threats and challenges they face. Therefore, staying informed and up-to-date is paramount.

We hope that this book bundle has provided readers with a holistic understanding of cloud security and forensics within Azure, AWS, and GCP. Whether you are just starting your cloud security journey or are already an expert in the field, there are valuable insights to be gained from these pages.

In closing, cloud security and forensics are not merely topics to be learned; they are ongoing journeys. The cloud will continue to shape the future of computing, and with it, the need for robust security and forensic practices. We encourage you to explore, experiment, and adapt as you navigate the ever-expanding landscape of cloud security and forensics.

Thank you for joining us on this journey, and we wish you success in securing and investigating the cloud environments of Azure, AWS, and GCP.